The New §1031 Handbook

Good News for Real Estate Investors

by
Bettye J. Matthews, CPA

authorHOUSE™

1663 LIBERTY DRIVE, SUITE 200
BLOOMINGTON, INDIANA 47403
(800) 839-8640
WWW.AUTHORHOUSE.COM

AuthorHouse™
1663 Liberty Drive, Suite 200
Bloomington, IN 47403
www.authorhouse.com
Phone: 1-800-839-8640

AuthorHouse™ UK Ltd.
500 Avebury Boulevard
Central Milton Keynes, MK9 2BE
www.authorhouse.co.uk
Phone: 08001974150

First published by AuthorHouse 3/6/2006

ISBN: 1-4208-8805-6 (e)
ISBN: 1-4208-8794-7 (sc)

Printed in the United States of America
Bloomington, Indiana

This book is printed on acid-free paper.

While this §1031 Handbook is designed to guide the investor through the 1031 process, it cannot be relied upon as "absolute" and may not be relied upon for legal or tax advice. Specific conditions may exist within an exchange that, when taken in their entirety, produce an indefensible situation with regard to U.S. Treasury Regulations.

For this reason, investors should always seek the council of their attorney, financial advisors, and accountants for a benefit analysis before entering into a §1031 exchange.

Forward

I have witnessed many "cookie cutter" seminars, training sessions dispensing recipes for exchanging investment real estate. But what happens when the ingredients for the recipe change or are not available? What do these seminars teach about substituting ingredients? Nothing.

In our experience, most Exchangers (taxpayers) begin with questions such as - what if.........., but then what...........? But in my case...........? You get the picture.

All properties for sale and purchase are not created equal. There are differences in structure, order and disorder. Ownership and title differences, shared ownerships, tenants-in-common, joint partnerships, and corporate properties all of which may combine to make each exchange unique.

Investors need a starting point and this handbook is just what the doctor ordered. The basic principles are revealed quickly to both new investors and those seasoned veterans in need of a quick review.

The IRS has established a "safe harbor" for both the standard forward and reverse exchanges. However, if you never untie your boat and venture out into and beyond the safe harbor you may never know how many opportunities exist.

If we always seek out the perfect unchallengeable path many good and fair exchanges can be missed.

By investing your time in this little big book [sic] you will open opportunities to real estate investment that you may not have considered.

For example, deferring capital gain tax and putting profit to work buying more investment property or buying that special property first to get it off the market and exchanging later. And consider using profit to leverage even more investment property.

Today's stock market presents an intimidating environment for investors. Many have turned to real estate to produce the highest and best use of their investment dollars in the foreseeable future.

Now for the good news - In a very real sense this handbook has been a labor of love because Bettye Matthews loves to teach. Bettye Matthews, CPA, developed a course on the "Effect of Taxation on Real Estate" while lecturing at the University of Maryland, University College, at College Park. During this period, she helped hundreds of licensed real estate brokers learn how to improve their transactions.

It was a natural progression that brings Ms. Matthews, this handbook and you together. Whether you are a real estate investor or thinking of becoming one, this is the place to start.

Warren R. Matthews,

Husband

Mr. & Ms. Matthews will celebrate their 44th wedding anniversary in October 2006. They have two married daughters and four grandchildren.

Table of Contents

Acknowledgement

I want to thank Arlene LaStella of Dunn Title Company in Naples, Florida who is an accounting and tax client as well as a dear friend. One day she asked me: "Hey Bet, what do you know about 1031 exchanges?"

Can you imagine trading New Amsterdam for Beads and Blankets?

When money had no value, "things" did......

When you were in Elementary School, you probably heard the story of Petr Styvesant purchasing Manhattan Island from the local Indians in exchange for some beads and blankets. Money did not change hands and so far as dealing with the North American Indian in the 16th Century, money had no value, things had value.

America's economy continued to move forward using a barter type system for many years. This was especially so in the Northwest Territory where animal pelts were the primary objects of value. Trappers trapped, middlemen traded food, blankets, guns etc. for the pelts. Eventually the pelts were sold to a furrier who made coats, hats and boots from the pelts and in turn sold the finished good to their customers.

Trading was and remains an integral part of our economy. Swapping pieces of land (real property) as well as items considered personal property was first included in the Internal Revenue Code (IRC) in the 1920's. Section 202 of the Revenue Act of 1921 contains a provision for the exchange of property (both real and personal) and allows the non-recognition of gain or loss. The original concept was for two or more property owners to simultaneously trade deeds or title to their property. There were no delayed trades as the regulations allow today. These simultaneous trades were difficult to accomplish because you had to locate someone who wanted the property you owned and who was willing to purchase property you wished to acquire and then trade with you. Many trades involved 3 or more parties; only one of which might be involved in a tax deferred exchange. In cases where the Fair Market Value (FMV) of the properties to be traded is unequal, cash or other property would be included to equalize the value. This cash or other property is called "Boot" and can cause problems even today. We will discuss the ramifications of boot in another chapter.

The primary rule that must be met for like-kind exchanges (whether personal property or real property) is:

Property included in a tax deferred exchange must be used in a trade or business or held for investment.

For property to be considered as qualifying for like-kind treatment, the rules are a little different when considering real or personal property.

For exchanges involving Real Property, we look to the use of the property in the hands of the exchanger. Is it rental property? Does the exchanger's business operate from the site? Is it vacant land, or pasture, or a farm? All of these properties are either held for investment or used in a trade or business and are interchangeable.

For Personal Property, the rules as to what is like-kind are more stringent. We must look to Standard Industrial Codes (SIC) or other asset class systems to determine if it is of like-kind and exchangeable. An easier way to think about personal property is "similar use". If the property is owned by a business, they must exchange other personal property for personal property of a similar use; i.e. office equipment for office equipment, furniture or fixtures for furniture or fixtures, etc.

Some types of personal property are collectibles (stamps, coins, dolls etc.) In 1997, the tax rules on the sale of collectibles changed substantially and the gain realized on the sale of collectibles is currently taxed at a flat 28%.

It is important that anyone entering into a tax deferred exchange have a clear understanding of the process, the help of their tax preparer and be aware of court decisions regarding exchanges especially those involving personal property.

So, just what is like-kind?

A rule of thumb:

Real Estate - Virtually all properties that are <u>not for personal use</u> are like-kind to each other.

Personal Property - Is required to meet a slightly higher standard called "similar use."

What Does an Exchange Accomplish?

The exchange process is really a basis substitution. The basis of the property relinquished is substituted, with adjustments, into the property acquired. You cannot have a basis greater than the fair market value of the property you acquired. If you acquire property of greater value than you gave up, a basis adjustment may be allowed depending on whether you gave other property or cash as "boot".

An Example:

Relinquished Property
To calculate realized gain immediately prior to the transfer of the relinquished property.

Selling Price	$125,000.
Purchase Price	-$75,000.
Closing Costs	- 3,750.
Depreciation	$34,000.
Gain (Profit)	$80,250.

Replacement Property
To calculate gain realized immediately after the acquisition of the replacement property.

Purchase Price	$150,000.
Basis Old (Net)	$44,750.
Increased Price	$25,000.
Basis New	$69,750.
Gain (Profit)	$80,250.

Notice how the basis in the relinquished property is substituted with adjustments as the basis in the new property. This allows the profit you accumulated while you owned the relinquished property to be transferred to the replacement property. It is this substitution that allows the deferral of Capital Gain Tax.

A couple of things are accomplished by doing a tax deferred exchange.

1. You can use all of the proceeds to acquire other property. You lose nothing   to taxes.

2. You can put off paying the tax required until another day. When you finally sell, you can pay the tax due in cheaper dollars (time value of money) or with patience, hard work and good planning never pay tax on the gain due to appreciation.

Is it Boot or Booty???

In case you are wondering about this word "boot", it appears to have several possible origins. One of which suggests that it comes from the days of sieges and piracy when soldiers and pirates received "extra value" for their hard work in the form of whatever "booty" they could find, steal, plunder or otherwise extract from their victims.

A second origin and perhaps more realistic and certainly less romantic is that boot represents throwaway property. Sort of like "one man's trash is another man's treasure". This other property would be used as an equalizer in an exchange of properties that were of unequal value. In this case, a deal would be struck where the giver "throws it in to boot" and the receiver get to "boot it around a bit".

Regardless of the origin, boot can be a real problem in an exchange. It is nearly always taxable.

If you get cash out of an exchange, it probably will be considered boot and the cash will be taxed accordingly.

An important thing about boot surfaces when discussing mortgages. The Internal Revenue Service (IRS) considers mortgages to be "other property" or cash and therefore boot. If a mortgage is paid off at the closing of your relinquished property using funds provided by your purchaser, you are considered to have received boot. The only way to offset the receipt of boot is to give boot. ***Thus, to avoid taxable boot, you are required to acquire a mortgage on the replacement property in an amount at least equal to the mortgage paid off on the property you sold.*** If the mortgage is decreased or non existent, you must bring "new" money (cash) to the exchange.

If you wish to reduce or have no mortgage on the replacement property by bringing new money to settlement on the replacement property, it will relieve you of the "mortgage boot" problem. Cash is cash boot and mortgage boot is other property which is sometimes a problem.

If you have the funds available and do not want to have a mortgage on the replacement property, you can pay the mortgage off prior to or at closing on the relinquished property.

Like Kind is not necessarily "Same Kind"

There is great detail within the law and the regulations about what like-kind is and is not. When trading personal property like automobiles, boats, tools, furniture, equipment, etc., the term becomes more exacting and similar use plays an important part.

To determine like-kind for personal property, you must look to the Standard Industrial Code (SIC) or a similar asset classification system to determine just how similar the use has to be. When trading real property (real estate) the lines are a lot less fuzzy.

In real estate, what would be property used in a trade or business? An auto repair business that owns the building in which it operates would qualify as property used in a trade or business. Some rental properties qualify as a trade or business if it is rented to transient travelers such as is the case with a hotel or motel.

Which Types of Property Are Considered Like-Kind?

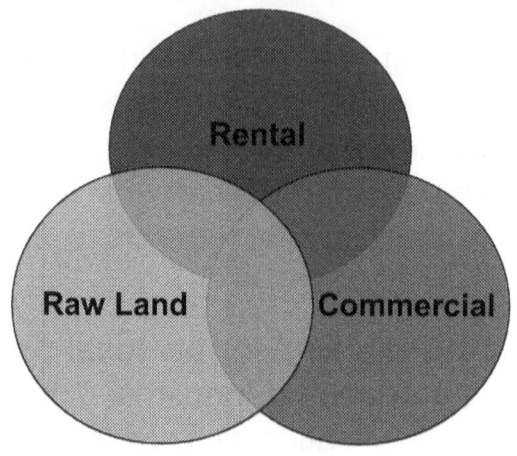

In the proper use, these are all interchangeable as Like-Kind Properties

Like-Kind Property

Raw Land / Farm Land

Commercial

Waterfront Condos

Condominium and
Office Suites

NOTE:

If exchanging a depreciable asset for non-depreciable asset (land with building for raw land) depreciation recapture may be required.

Any of these investment properties can be traded for any other investment property. It does not have to be the same or even similar use.

The real estate only has to be investment property or property used in a trade or business in the hands of the taxpayer considering a tax deferred exchange.

However, you cannot trade a property for improvements to be made on other property *you already own*. Many investors want to build a rental dwelling on property they already own. Their desire is to exchange a property and use the proceeds to build improvements on a vacant lot they already own. **This does not meet the requirements of a like-kind exchange.**

We have to look to another section of the Income Tax Code (§ 1033) for an explanation of why this will not be acceptable. Even though IRS §1033 deals with involuntary conversions of property to money, it contains the underlying language for replacement property. The section allows for tax deferral on property sold under condemnation or threat of condemnation and for property destroyed by fire, theft or other disaster. Some very special treatment is allowed under these circumstances that permit the taxpayer time (up to three years) to replace or rebuild property lost or damaged due the circumstances beyond their control.

The caveat when dealing with real estate and Tax Deferred Exchanges is that you must replace dirt with dirt.

Land lost to condemnation must be replaced with other land. When applying the "dirt for dirt" rule, trading land for an improvement on other land you already own simply does not qualify.

The law and the regulations are clear on other kinds of property that will not qualify for like-kind treatment. Among them are:

- ☛ Inventory or other stock in trade

- ☛ Stocks, bonds or notes

- ☛ Other securities or evidences of indebtedness or interest

- ☛ Interests in a partnership

- ☛ Certificates of Trust or Beneficial Interests

- ☛ Choses in action

Trailblazers of a New Frontier
In Real Estate

As mentioned earlier, the concept of trading assets was originally thought to only occur as a simultaneous trade. There were no delayed exchanges and the regulations did not require that an identification of the replacement property be made within a specific time frame. In addition, the regulations did not specify an ending to the exchange period other than to say that the exchange was complete when replacement property was acquired or on the filing of the exchanger's tax return plus extensions. This left a lot of room for some imaginative transactions.

In July, 1967, the Starker Family (father, son and daughter-in-law) entered into an agreement to trade timberland they owned jointly to Crown Zellerbach for other land to be identified and transferred to them within 5 years. Crown Zellerbach agreed to pay cash for any land that was not transferred to the Starkers at the end of 5 years. Furthermore, Crown Zellerbach agreed to credit the Starker' accounts with a growth factor of 6% at the end of each year.

At the time, the Starkers didn't know which parcels of land they wanted to acquire, but they did know the location of the parcels would be in Oregon or Washington State. The son, Bruce and his wife, Elizabeth, located their replacement property in just four months. Crown Zellerbach purchased that property and transferred it to the younger Starkers, thus closing their portion of the exchange. T. J. Starker (the father) took nearly two years to identify and acquire 12 parcels of land he wished to receive. At the time, there was nothing within the tax law that specifically prohibited this type of transaction.

In fact exchanges, as contemplated by the Internal Revenue Service (IRS), were thought to apply only to simultaneous transfers of deeds at a single settlement. The younger Starkers completed their exchange early on and filed their tax return deferring all gain on the land transactions. The IRS disagreed with their interpretation of §1031 and issued a notice of deficiency and requested payment of taxes which were due on the sale of land. The tax was paid and a refund claim was filed.

The son and his wife's claim eventually wound up in court. It became known as Starker I. In this instance, the court agreed with the Starkers and found for them. The IRS appealed the decision but later withdrew their appeal allowing the decision to stand.

The father's tax return was filed when the exchange was completed. Again the IRS disagreed with the taxpayer's interpretation of §1031. He also paid the assessed tax and filed a claim for refund. This case also found its way into court. It is known as Starker II. The same judge was involved in both cases. In the father's case, the judge found for the IRS and believed he had erred in his finding for the younger Starkers. The same defenses and arguments were used in both cases.

Eventually, Starker II found its way to the appellate court. This court ruled in favor of the taxpayer (Starker) on every point except the transfer of one of the replacements properties. In that case, Mr. Starker had the parcel deeded to his daughter. That parcel was held to be not of a like-kind because of the deeding.

Most of the success of Starker II lies in the fact that the IRS withdrew its appeal in Starker I. Essentially, the IRS agreed that the exchange methods used in Starker I were acceptable. Most of the properties acquired by the father used the same exchange method the son had used.

These cases reached their conclusion (1977) some 10 years after the exchanges began.

During the period the Starker exchanges were being decided and for about 15 years afterward, there was some very creative exchange activity taking place. Just a glance at the numbers of court cases, Revenue Rulings, Revenue Procedures and Field Advisories will give you a pretty good idea of the level of activity that was being challenged by the Internal Revenue Service.

By 1991, the Internal Revenue Service was successful in drafting legislation establishing the guidelines currently used for like-kind exchanges.

While taxpayers may still trade properties without involving an intermediary, they can engage attorneys to arrange the required paperwork and in a simultaneous trade and recording of deeds by two or more parties engaged in a like-kind exchange.

Safe Harbor, 1991

However, the "safe harbor" created by Congress in 1991 has made exchanging property much easer and considerably less expensive for taxpayers.

The Delayed Tax Deferred Exchange and How It Works

These are the true "Starker Exchanges". The taxpayer (exchanger) wishes to change his real estate holdings for other properties that better suit their investment goals. They may want to change the geographical location of the property, or the type of investment property.

Under the current rules, the taxpayer contracts with a realtor, if they wish to use one, to sell the property in question. When an executed contract of sale is complete, the taxpayer should engage an intermediary or other 'safe harbor' to act as the facilitator of the exchange.

There are three other safe harbors available to the taxpayer, however, we believe the intermediary is the easiest method for the exchanger; creates the least problems and requires little effort on the part of the exchanger or their Realtor. *It is important that the contract to sell include a paragraph that states that the seller intends the transaction to be part of a Tax Deferred Exchange and that the purchaser agrees to cooperate.* This paragraph alone clearly establishes's the taxpayer's intent to enter into the 1031 exchange process.

Usually the qualified intermediary will insert additional wording that the purchaser will incur no additional costs nor will closing be delayed as a result of the exchange process.

When the exchanger has selected an intermediary for the exchange, they will have to provide some basic information such as name, address, phone, social security number (for reporting interest), a copy of the contract of sale and a copy of the deed showing the current titleholders, and the closing agent along with their phone number.

This information allows the intermediary to prepare the exchange agreement, an assignment of the sale contract and closing instructions for the title company or attorney who will be closing the transaction.

The exchanger should now focus their interest on selecting the replacement property. Remember, only 45 days from the closing date can pass before the replacement property must be identified. To take advantage of the exchange process, the replacement property search should begin once the exchanger has decided a Tax Deferred Exchange is his best course of action.

If you cannot deliver a signed purchase contract containing 1031 language to the intermediary within the 45 day identification period, you will be required to complete an identification form.

When you have an executed purchase contract for the replacement property, a copy of this contract along with the name and phone number of your title company or closing attorney must be forwarded to your intermediary so that an assignment of contract and closing instructions can be prepared.

When the property you are selling is transferred to your buyer, the mortgage, if any, will be paid off at closing and any proceeds will be forwarded to your intermediary.

Normally, the intermediary will put those funds in an interest bearing escrow account and forward them to your replacement closing.

A more detailed discussion of the exchange process is in a later chapter.

Who can Provide Intermediary Services?

The law and the regulations are written in such a manner that anyone can be an intermediary. A Qualified Intermediary (QI) is merely a person who is not a disqualified person.

The law is very specific on who a disqualified person is. Generally a disqualified person is any person that has acted as an agent of the taxpayer at anytime in the 24 months prior to the beginning of the exchange period.

Typically, disqualified persons are:

- The taxpayer

- Family members

- Employees

- The taxpayer's Attorney

- The taxpayer's Accountant or tax preparer

- The taxpayer's Broker or Banker

- The taxpayer's Realtor or Real Estate the Agent

- Any corporation, partnership or other entity in which the taxpayer/s has a 10% or greater share interest

A disqualified person is not allowed to act as an escrow agent and cannot receive an identification of replacement property.

The reason great care must be taken to avoid involving a disqualified person is the issue of **constructive receipt**. (See the next chapter)

Our experience indicates that the intermediary should have detailed knowledge of the workings of §1031 including enough experience to foresee potential problem areas.

Therefore, we believe a qualified intermediary who can perform well for you should have an excellent knowledge of §1031 as well as other areas of the tax code that impinge on Tax Deferred Exchanges. This person should be a professional in the legal or tax accounting field or be a designated Certified Exchange Specialist.*

(CES)*

Certified Exchange Specialist (CES) is a certification program sponsored by the Federation of Exchange Accommodators (FEA). This program sets standards for education and work experience. Candidates must pass a nationally standardized test and endorse the ethics rules established buy the FEA.

What is Constructive Receipt?

Constructive receipt occurs when you have dominion and control over the proceeds from the sale of the relinquished property. This is a touchy subject. The exchange agreement should state unequivocally that you have no control or access to the funds. In addition, you cannot pledge them as collateral on an unrelated financial matter.

A simpler explanation of constructive receipt goes something like this. It is the end of the year and you are a cash basis taxpayer as are most individuals. You operate a business which you report with a Schedule C within your personal tax return. You have had a good business year and are looking for ways to decrease you income for the year. You decide to delay depositing receipts in you bank account until the first of next year. This is constructive receipt. You have control over when the deposit will be made. Legally all the revenue you are holding and planning to deposit next year should be included in the current year's tax return.

You can inadvertently acquire dominion and control just by directing your settlement officer to cut you a check for $10,000.00 from the proceeds of sale. You know the $10,000 is taxable but you could wind up having the exchange nullified by giving this type of direction and actually receiving the funds. You can also acquire dominion and control by directing your settlement officer to pay off an equity line on property that is unrelated to the relinquished property.

In a recent case, the IRS found that a taxpayer had constructive receipt of his replacement property (reverse exchange) even though he had used an accommodator for the acquisition. He purchased the property with a mortgage, but failed to include the accommodator on the mortgage as an additional borrower (Declenes v. commissioner.)

In another instance the Court ruled that an exchange was a sale and a purchase because the exchanger received funds from the exchange credits before the exchange period had ended. This ruling actually negated an exchange of properties that had occurred. The Court determined from the facts and circumstances that the exchanger had dominion and control over the funds from the beginning. (Florida Industries v. commissioner)

Great care must be taken to avoid constructive receipt of the funds in a forward exchange or the replacement property in a reverse exchange.

The Exchange Process

The exchange process should begin with a frank discussion between you and your tax preparer, attorney or financial planner.

Once you have determined that an exchange is in your best interest, you should locate a Qualified Intermediary who will guide you through the process.

Generally, the exchanger should begin looking for their replacement property immediately upon making a decision to sell their investment property. It may not be necessary to pin down a specific parcel, but the general location and type of real estate should be established early on in the process.

The intermediary will provide the exchanger with an exchange agreement, which sets out the terms of their contract (agreement). Some important components included in the agreement:

1) The agreement provides for the assignment of both the sale and purchase agreements (contracts).

2) Includes a provision that limits the exchanger's access to the proceeds of the sale of the relinquished property. This includes the ability to pledge the proceeds as collateral in an unrelated transaction.

3) Includes a provision regarding the Growth Factor (interest) on the sale proceeds while in the hands of the intermediary.

4) Includes a provision for identifying the replacement property, the possible revocation of that identification and the re-identification of other replacement property.

5) Includes a provision for when the exchanger may gain access to unused sale proceeds in the event the exchange is not completed or if there are excess proceeds.

6) Includes a provision discussing the method of deeding both the relinquished property and the replacement property. Usually a Direct Deed process is used which treats the transfer as if the intermediary were included in the deeding process.

7) Includes the responsibilities of the exchanger.

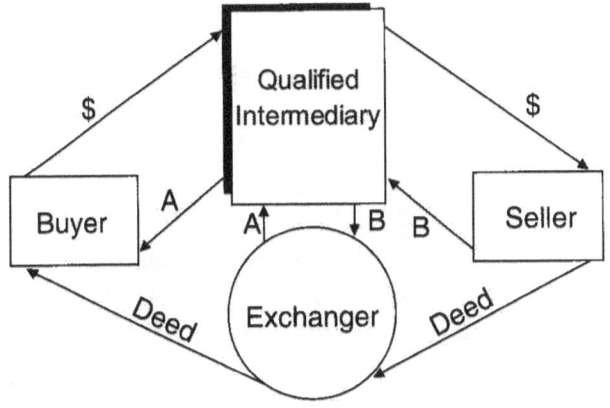

Diagram Key

A represents contract between exchanger, Intermediary and the buyer of the relinquished property.

B represents contracts related to replacement property.

8) Includes the duties of the intermediary.

9) Includes a provision that the exchanger assumes all risk.

10) Includes a provision regarding the independent status of the intermediary; that an agency relationship does not exist and the taxpayer (exchanger) has sought their own legal and/or tax advice.

The money is held by the intermediary

Earned interest generally goes to the exchanger

The intermediary will also provide an assignment of the sale contract in which the exchanger assigns their interest in the contract to the intermediary for the purpose of effecting a Section 1031 exchange. As part of the assignment process, a notice of assignment is also included which is to be signed by the exchanger. The notice is provided to the purchaser of the property and their signature will be requested as required by the Internal Revenue Code.

Most of the time, these documents are signed just prior to the property transfer at closing.

Speaking of closing, the intermediary should also provide the closing officer a set of instructions describing the closing process and the method of deeding. In a forward, 'Starker' type exchange, a direct deed is used. This term is used because both the exchange agreement and the closing instructions specifically require a direct deed but stipulates that the deed will be treated as if the property were deeded from the exchanger to the intermediary and from the intermediary to the purchaser.

The use of a direct deed is used to transfer the deed directly from the seller to the buyer. If the deed were to actually pass through the hands of the intermediary additional transfer tax, recording fees or other state and local charges on real estate transfers would have to be paid. Most states and local governments accept the direct deed process. One or two do not, so make sure you understand the local rules for the towns, cities, and counties in which your property is located.

The closing instructions usually require the closing office to secure signatures on the exchange agreement, assignment(s) and notice(s) of assignment prior to the actual closing on the property transfer. This is because the exchange process must begin prior to the property transfer.

In addition to the deeding information, the closing instructions will contain information on how the settlement statement is to be worded. The intermediary should be shown as an additional seller/buyer and proceeds of sale must go to the intermediary. The instructions will also give direction for forwarding the proceeds to the intermediary.

The exchange period which can run a maximum of 180 days begins on the date of the first transfer of property to be included in the exchange. In a forward (Starker type) exchange this would be on the day the first relinquished property closes. In the case of a reverse exchange, the exchange begins when the accommodator's Exchange Accommodation Titleholder (EAT) take title to either the Relinquished or the Replacement property.

Important points about the exchange process:

☛ The Identification period is imbedded within the Exchange Period

☛ The identification period runs concurrently with exchange period and has a maximum duration of 45 days.

☛ Both periods end at midnight on the 180th or 45th day whichever applies.

☛ Neither the exchange period nor the identification period qualifies for an extension of time unless the property is located in a presidentially declared "Disaster Area". (See the discussion for Disaster relief in the next section)

The Exchange Period Timeline

The exchanger has 180 days from the close of the relinquished property to complete the exchange. By the 45th day, the replacement property must be identified in writing.

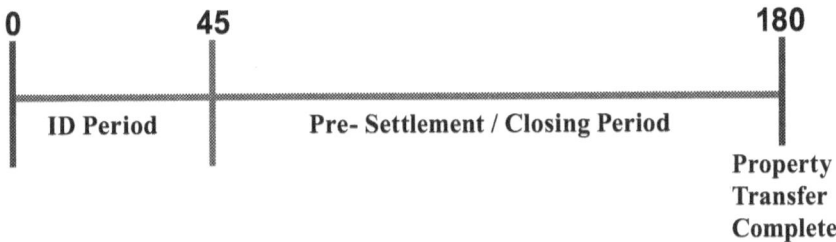

It is important to plan ahead So that your exchange will be free of worry and frustrations.

Are Extensions to the Time Lines Allowed?   Is one Available?

Generally, NO!   There is no mechanism for the exchanger to request an extension of either the identification period or the exchange period.

However, in the autumn of 2004, the Internal Revenue Service put in place a method for determining if an extension of either or both time lines was applicable to a specific exchange.

If either the relinquished or replacement property is located within a Presidentially declared Disaster Area which cause the settlement of property to be delayed, or the identified property to be damaged or destroyed, the exchanger will receive a 120 extension of time to identify additional property or to close on property previously identified.

It is necessary for your tax preparer to write the name of the disaster in bold red letters in the top margin of form 8824 to justify the longer than normal identification period or exchange period.

To Whom May I Sell My Property?

You can sell your relinquished property to anyone you choose who is a qualified buyer and will follow through with actual closing and transfer of title.

However, if you contract to sell to or buy from a related party, there are restrictions regarding what the family member or you the exchanger can do with the property. Remember, in the hands of the purchaser, use is not an issue but when the purchaser is a family member or other related party, the property cannot be sold for the 24 month period following the transaction. Similarly, if you purchase the replacement property from a related party, you cannot dispose of the property during the 24 month period following the transaction. If you dispose of the property, the Internal Revenue Service may challenge the exchange and declare it a sale and therefore taxable.

To follow up on this, the Internal Revenue Service requires the purchaser and or seller as well as the exchanger to file form 8824 (like-kind exchanges) with the Internal Revenue Service for the year of the exchange and for a 2 year period following the year of the exchange.

A related person is any person related to you within the definition described in the tax law. Generally, it includes siblings, parents, grandparents, children, grandchildren, foster children, adopted children, nieces or nephews, aunts or uncles or any other person with a direct ancestral or descendent relationship to you or your spouse. It also includes any entity in which the exchanger or their spouse holds a 10% or greater interest. Related party rules are also extended to include partnerships, corporations or LLCs that have common owners.

<u>Don't</u> plan your exchange without carefully considering the effects of family members and close business associates.

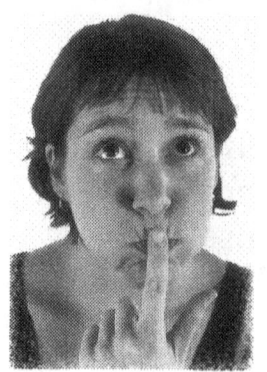

From Whom May I Purchase My Property?

You can purchase your replacement property from anyone you choose who is willing to sell and will follow through with actual closing and transfer of title.

However, if you contract to buy from or sell to a related party, there are restrictions regarding what you can do with the property. Remember, in the hands of the seller, use is not an issue but when the seller is a family member, the property cannot be resold or exchanged for the 24 month period following the transaction. If you dispose of the property, the Internal Revenue Service may challenge the exchange and declare it a sale and therefore taxable.

To follow up on this, the Internal Revenue Service requires the purchaser and or seller as well as the exchanger to file form 8824 (like-kind exchanges) with the Internal Revenue Service for the year of the exchange and for a 2 year period following the year of the exchange.

A related person is any person related to you within the definition described in the tax law. Generally, it includes siblings, parents, grandparents, children, grandchildren, foster children, adopted children, nieces or nephews, aunts or uncles or any other person with a direct ancestral or descendent relationship to you or your spouse. It also includes any entity in which the exchanger or their spouse holds a 10% or greater interest. Related party rules are also extended to include partnerships, corporations or LLCs that have common owners.

More on Related Parties...

Under some new rulings regarding related parties, it is also important to show that the purpose for the exchange was not to change low basis property into higher basis property. This can happen and usually the Internal Revenue Service will declare the exchange a sale and purchase because of the abusive nature of the basis substitution.

In a recent case two LLCs with common members exchanged property with a third unrelated party. The LLC that eventually recorded the transaction as a sale and elected to recognize the gain also had substantial carryover capital losses. These losses more than covered the gain recognized on the real estate transaction. The court held that the exchange was structured for tax avoidance purposes. The exchange was declared a sale and purchase and therefore voided.

How do I identify my Replacement Property?

You are required to identify your replacement property as unambiguously as possible. Usually the legal description is best but often the mailing address will suffice so long as the mailing address cannot be confused with any other parcel. If a unit number applies, it must be included.

You can revoke your identification at any time during the identification period. However, whatever property that is identified as of midnight on the 45th day of the exchange period is the only property that will be considered like-kind for replacement property purposes.

A proper revocation is necessary if you decide during the identification period that you do not wish to proceed with the exchange. Under the rules and regulations of §1031, the exchanger may have access to the relinquished proceeds only under certain conditions:

1) At the end of the 45 day identification period if a proper identification has not been made.

2) If all properly identified property has been acquired and the identification period has expired.

3) After the end of the exchange period (180 days) if a proper identification has been made and all of the identified property has not been acquired.

4) A material and substantial contingency has occurred that is directly related to the exchange and is beyond the exchanger's control.

As you go through the identification process, keep in mind that regulations are in place that prohibits your qualified intermediary from returning any unused exchange proceeds (credits) to you if you have identified property that you have not yet received. Unfortunately, this applies to the three property rule where your intention is to acquire only one of the three properties. If there are funds still being held by the intermediary after you have closed on the replacement property, you will have to wait until the end of the exchange period to receive those funds. Read your agreement with the intermediary carefully, you should find language that limits your ability to receive funds prior to the end of the exchange period.

How Many Properties May I Identify?

There are 3 tiers of identification rules. The lowest level and least complicated is called the 3 property rule. This rule allows you to identify up to 3 properties without regard to their aggregate value.

The rule works in this way:
Your relinquished property sold for $150,000.

You may identify up to 3 properties:
1 valued at $150,000.
1 valued at $175,000.
1 valued at $190,000.

You may close on any one of these properties or all three of the properties and be able to complete a like-kind exchange provided you meet the rules on boot including mortgage boot.

The second tier for identification is called the 200% rule and it works like this:

If you identify more than three (3) properties, their estimated aggregate value cannot exceed 200% of the value of the relinquished property or more simply put; twice its value.

An example of identifications using the 200% rule would look like the following:

Your relinquished property sold for $150,000.
You identify 5 properties:

 1 value estimated at$25,000.
 1 value estimated at$30,000.
 1 value estimated at$35,000.
 1 value estimated at$60,000.
 1 value estimated at$150,000.

You may close on any combination of the identified properties. Of course, if you fail to close on at least $150,000 of value you may be subject to capital gain tax on the portion you did not reinvest.

Finally, even if you exceed the 200% rule there is a third tier at which the property you acquire can still be considered like-kind. This rule is referred to as the 95% rule and is generally a tough standard to meet. This rule requires that you close on and actually acquire 95% of the aggregate value of the property you have identified. To meet this level, be prepared to provide "new" money or to seriously leverage the acquired property.

Your relinquished property sold for $150,000.

You identify multiple properties which exceed both the 3 property rule and the 200% rule.

You Identify 4 properties:

 1 value estimated at $125,000.
 1 value estimated at $150,000.
 1 value estimated at $160,000.
 1 value estimated at $100,000.

There a 4 identified properties whose estimated aggregate value is $535,000. Any of these 4 properties that are actually acquired within the 45 day identification period will be included in the exchange regardless of any other property you acquire or fail to acquire. For any property you acquire after the end of the 45 day identification period to qualify as like-kind, you will have to acquire 95% of the aggregate value of all identified property or $413,250. This is a unique situation but very real and at times very painful. In this situation the only property that is not required to be purchased is property #4. Because the 95% rule is in effect, you would have to spend $435,000 on replacement property to protect the gain on the $150,000 sale from being taxed.

Occasionally an exchanger will decide not to proceed once they become aware they are going to have to work with the 95% rule. They believe that since the Internal Revenue Service treats the excessive identifications as if nothing has been identified the exchange is over and they are entitled to receive their proceeds. However, that is not the case because the regulations require that the fair market value of the properties be established at the time of closing or **at the end of the exchange period.**

A couple of words of caution when identifying property that is not under contract. First, if your prospective seller becomes aware that you have identified his property as replacement property and the identification period had ended, don't be surprised if your ability to negotiate becomes very limited. While it is a requirement that all parties involved in a §1031 exchange be informed that the transaction is intended to qualify for tax deferral it is not necessary that the seller of replacement property be notified immediately upon introduction.

Second, the Internal Revenue Service does not recognize an inability to negotiate an executable contract as sufficient reason to release funds to the exchanger prior to the 180th day unless the exchange agreement stipulates such a release of funds. Most intermediaries will not agree to such a stipulation because it exposes all of their exchanges to audit as well as exposing any completed portion of your exchange to gain recognition and therefore taxation. See the comment regarding Florida Industries v. commissioner in the appendix for Case Studies.

Once the property to be relinquished is transferred to the purchaser, you are free to close on the property you intend to acquire any time in the next 180 days.

When the exchanger has an executed contract to purchase replacement property, the same procedure is followed as when the sale agreement was executed. Provide a copy of the purchase contract to the intermediary who will, in turn, provide the required assignment, notice of assignment and closing instructions to the closing officer.

It is important to keep in mind for exchanges whose exchange period began late in the calendar year and can reasonably be expected to extend beyond April 15 (the due date for filing the tax return for the tax year in which the exchange period began). Do not file your tax return for the year the exchange period began until the replacement property has been received.

If it is your desire to complete the exchange, you must file for an automatic extension of the filing date. Filing an extension for filing a tax return does not extend the due date for paying whatever taxes may be due.

If you mistakenly file the tax return, the exchange period will have ended on the date of filing and any property you receive after the filing date will not be considered of like-kind. Essentially, the transaction that relinquished your property becomes a sale; any gain realized will have to be recognized and taxes may be due.

Do not file your tax return until the exchange is complete. The entire exchange must be reported in the same tax year.

Finally, if you fail to identify any property or if your identification is inappropriate, you will not be able to receive your proceeds until the end of the exchange period unless the exchange agreement specifically says you may have access to the proceeds under certain circumstances and clearly defines those circumstances.

Most exchange agreements will stipulate that funds are available to the exchanger on the 46th day of the exchange period if a valid identification is not made.

Can I Spend More for my Replacement Property?

Indeed, in order to defer all proposed capital gain tax you must replace your property with property of equal or greater value. So, if you sell for $100,000 you should replace with a property you purchase for $100,000 or more. Closing costs produce adjustments in basis but are not necessarily deducted from the selling price to produce a net selling price. Sales commission you paid is always deducted when estimating how much must be spent to defer all taxes.

So, spending more is never a problem, spending less could cause some capital gain to be recognized and therefore taxes to be paid on the difference in the two values.

Earlier, we discussed "boot" and described it as other property or cash that is given and or taken during the exchange process. The Internal Revenue Service considers mortgages to be other property or cash and therefore "boot". If a mortgage exists on the property being relinquished and that mortgage is paid off using funds supplied by your buyer, then, in order to defer all capital gain tax you must acquire a purchase money mortgage of the same or greater value must be in place at the time the replacement property is acquired.

However, if you want a larger mortgage, make sure it is not so large that it causes the intermediary or the closing agent to disburse funds to you at the time you close on the replacement property or at the end of the exchange. Any funds going to you could be suspect and cause questions to be asked. If a deposit reimbursement is due you, ask the intermediary to reimburse the deposit in a single check so that the purpose for the check is clearly understood.

An Important Lesson to Remember For a Fully Tax Deferred Exchange:

Selling Price $\leq$ Purchase Price
Mortgage Relieved $\leq$ Mortgage Acquired
Relinquished Equity $\leq$ Replacement Equity

The taxpayer's economic condition cannot be improved upon as a direct result of the exchange.

The Reverse Exchange ....
How it Works

Perhaps the most important thing to remember about exchanging is that you must exchange "dirt for dirt". You cannot use the proceeds from a property you already own to improve another property you also own. Therefore, it is important when considering a reverse exchange that you **never** hold title to both the relinquished and the replacement properties at the same time.

The reverse exchange works very much the same as the forward exchange except in reverse. The most common type of reverse exchange is called the Reverse Last Exchange because the actual exchange of properties occurs last in the process. The reverse process:

1) You close on the replacement property first.

2) Instead of an Intermediary, you use a qualified accommodator. It is generally the same person or company.

3) Instead of an Exchange Agreement, you use a Qualified Accommodation Agreement

4) The intermediary or accommodator will identify an Exchange Accommodator Titleholder (EAT) to hold title to the replacement property. The EAT is usually an LLC or some other type of special purpose entity. The contracts to

purchase and sell properties must still be assigned to the intermediary/accommodator who will prepare notices of assignment and closing instructions for the closing agents.

You still have only 45 days to identify the property you intend to relinquish. Usually this is not a problem because the qualified accommodation agreement clearly and unambiguously identifies the relinquished property. But, if you are undecided on which of your properties you wish to relinquish you have only 45 days to make that decision. If for some reason you wish to change your identification, you may do so at any time within the first 45 days of the exchange period. You accomplish this by revoking any identification you have made and identifying another property you wish to dispose of.

In a safe-harbor reverse exchange, you also have 180 days to complete the exchange. Failure to complete the exchange within 180 days will result in your owning two properties, neither of which will qualify as like-kind property to each other.

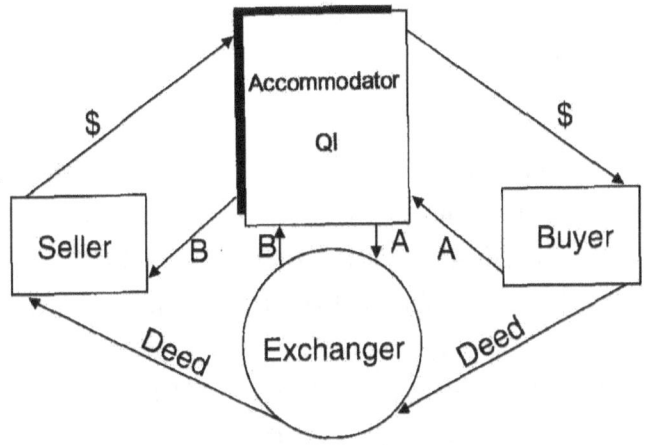

Diagram Key

A represents contract between exchanger, Intermediary and the buyer of the relinquished property.

B represents contracts related to replacement property.

If for some reason, you are approaching the end of the 180 day period and have not transferred ownership of the relinquished property you may have to work out an arrangement with the accommodator for a non-safe-harbor exchange.

In a non-safe-harbor exchange, the accommodator will have to have more indices of ownership. This means the accommodator will have to show that they have the benefits and burdens of ownership. For instance, the accommodator will have to actually pay the cost of any insurance, taxes or maintenance requirements that present themselves. The accommodator may require the exchanger to lease the replacement property and pay rent for the use of the property. The accommodator will have to include the revenues and expenses generated by the ownership on their tax return.

One very significant difference, and one that makes the reverse exchange considerably more expensive, is that the Qualified Accommodator becomes the titleholder of the replacement property until the relinquished property transaction is closed. Usually at the time of the closing of the relinquished property or shortly after, the Qualified Accommodator will transfer title of the replacement property to the exchanger.

Because the Internal Revenue Service requires that this transfer be for value, a quit claim deed will not meet the criteria. A full real estate closing must take place. This could mean additional documentary stamps, title insurance and possibly transfer taxes depending on the locality of the property.

It is not unusual for the Qualified Accommodator to charge a higher fee for the reverse exchange because there is exposure to liability as a result of being the titleholder and of course the additional challenges of owning property not the least of which is the number of documents which must handled by property owners. Most Qualified Accommodators will establish separate corporations or LLCs for the purpose of holding title in reverse exchanges.

Another cost, though hidden, with the reverse exchange is that the proceeds of sale earn no interest in this type of exchange since there is a near simultaneous transfer of the replacement property for the relinquished property. If the exchanger acquired a mortgage to purchase the replacement property, the Qualified Accommodator will use the proceeds to repay or buy down the principal amount of the mortgage to even up the mortgage boot. If the exchanger advanced new money in order to purchase the replacement property, the accommodator will refund the exchange proceeds to the exchanger at the time the replacement property is transferred to the exchanger.

Review Case Study III for a method for stringing two exchanges together and having almost a full year to complete your plan.

Why Consider a Reverse Exchange?

There are several reasons you might want to consider a reverse exchange. First, you found the property you want to acquire. The price is right and it won't be on the market long. Your long term investment strategy heavily favors this property and the seller wants a quick closing.

Example:

You found a property that will fit your investment goals that is ½ the price of the single family rental property you wish to relinquish. The new property is a 3 ½ story house that can be converted into three 2-bedroom apartments and 2 studios. This will go a long way toward the retirement nest egg. In addition, the rents will more than meet your immediate requirement for a positive cash flow.

Another reason, the property you want is real cheap but needs work to make it rentable. That is alright because you want to convert it to apartments anyway. This is a perfect way to take advantage of the reverse exchange.

You can arrange to purchase the property through a Qualified Accommodator. The Accommodation Agreement can include a clause regarding renovations and allow you to manage the property during the exchange period. The agreement could give you the responsibility of approving and signing renovation contracts with contractors. You must supply the funds for the purchase and the renovations until the relinquished property is sold. The Accommodator will pay the renovation costs from the funds you provided and the proceeds from the sale of the relinquished property.

The Accommodation Agreement will usually require a full accounting of revenue and expenses during the exchange period, so be prepared to provide a full detailed report. If there be a profit during the exchange period, a management fee should more than consume that. Remember, any management fee you receive is taxable income.

What is nice about the Reverse Improvement Exchange is that the property will transfer to the exchanger at the time the relinquished property is closed or later if extensive renovations are necessary. The Accommodator cannot hold the property more than 180 days and remain within the safe harbor. What makes this nice is that the value of the replacement property will be its value when the accommodator transfers it to you. By doing a reverse improvement exchange, it is possible to finance the improvements with proceeds from the sale of the relinquished property.

The proceeds can also be used to reduce the principle of any mortgage that was acquired to purchase and/or renovate the replacement property. Keep in mind, when the exchange is completed, the mortgages must be balanced or you may have some taxable gain.

Another situation which can be solved using a reverse exchange: you'd rather build on a vacant lot - no problem, if the construction can be far enough along in the 180 days allowed to give you the tax deferral you are looking for. Considerations of weather and ability of the builder to perform must be taken into account since there are no extensions available (other than a presidentially proclaimed disaster) if the construction is not far enough along.

The reverse improvement or construction exchange is best accomplished by purchasing the lot in the name of the accommodator and then commence construction immediately. If permitting, clearing, zoning or a variance is necessary it is not likely that much will be accomplished within the 180 day period. With the seller's written approval, permitting can often be accomplished before closing on the replacement property.

It is not unusual for permitting to take several months by itself. Zoning can take several years. Getting a variance from a local government can be time consuming as well.

Another method for acquiring property to be constructed where the acquisition and construction will require more than 180 days is to consider a forward exchange where the accommodator will (using your money) purchase the land, arrange for construction and when the new construction is within 180 days of completion go ahead with the closing of your relinquished property. When the construction is completed, the accommodator will transfer the property to you in a sale transaction. The promissory notes for the money you loaned the accommodator are cancelled in exchange for the newly constructed property at the time of settlement. Any funds left from the relinquished proceeds will be used to pay down a mortgage if necessary or refunded to you.

In some regions where it is customary for the builder to finance the construction, the same process previously discussed will work quite well. When the builder is within 180 days of completing the construction, the relinquished property should be closed and the proceeds held by the intermediary until the builder is ready to close.

Great care must be taken when purchasing property to be constructed where the builder is financing the construction. A builder probably will not close prior to the issuing of a certificate of occupancy. So, always allow time for the unexpected.

Finally, there is the reverse exchange that becomes necessary because of time constraints. You have a contract on your relinquished property and you have signed a contract to purchase the replacement property. Your buyer fails to perform. Yes, you may have legal remedies, and so will the seller of your replacement property if you fail to close on your contract. A reverse can solve the problem, while you look for another buyer for your relinquished property.

There are Two Types of Reverse Exchanges

Exchange First and Exchange Last

When you determine that a reverse exchange is necessary to meet your investment goals, there is still another decision to make.

Which property do I want the accommodator to hold: the relinquished or the replacement?

There are reasons that you might want to pick one over the other.

Reason #1 - If you need a mortgage to close on the replacement property, make sure the lender knows that you are doing a reverse 1031 exchange and that the accommodator will hold the title for a short period. My experience has shown that many lenders will not permit the property to be titled in a name other than that of the borrower. Typically, the accommodator will allow their name to be on the mortgage document which allows the lender to place a lien on the property. The accommodator will sign this since it is the titleholder. But the accommodator may not be willing to sign the promissory note which guarantees repayment. Some lenders will require the accommodator to sign the note as well. When that is required, the accommodator will want to set up a new LLC (or other special purpose entity) to be the titleholder. When it is time to transfer the property to the exchanger, the membership in the LLC will be transferred to you. Special care must be taken to avoid creating a partnership by transferring a single member LLC to a husband and wife. If the relinquished property is held by more than one person i.e. husband and wife, a separate LLC must be formed for each individual. Each of the two LLCs will hold a 50% undivided interest in the replacement property. Membership in the one LLC will be transferred to each titleholder on the relinquished property for their respective undivided interest.

Reason #2 – Some lenders sill not lend funds when the titleholder is an LLC or other special purpose entity.

Reason #3 - Some states or regions do not recognize 1031 exchanges for transfer tax purposes. Where this is true, you will want the accommodator to hold the property that incurs the least transfer tax.

Reason #4 - Sometimes the relinquished property does not close on time and the normally planned for 'Starker' type exchange becomes a reverse because the seller of the replacement property requires you to close as stipulated in the contract to purchase. Documents for this closing are already drawn up. Mortgage underwriters don't like sudden changes no matter what the cause and they could withdraw their approval. Both the lender and the title company will probably charge redraw fees which could be substantial.

The two types of reverse exchanges reflect the timing of the transfer of the relinquished property. If you transfer the relinquished property to the accommodator, the exchange is considered an exchange first. The actual exchange, from the exchanger's point of view has occurred early on in the exchange process because the relinquished property was transferred to the accommodator and later in the same day or the next day; the exchanger acquired the replacement property.

If the exchanger elects to hold onto the relinquished property and allow the accommodator to acquire the replacement property, the exchange is considered to be an exchange last. The actual exchange will not be completed until after the relinquished property is sold. The accommodator will transfer the replacement property and the proceeds (after making any required principle curtailment) will go to the exchanger.

And the Newest Kid on the Block?? Tenancy in Common (TICs)

Earlier in this handbook, we said that partnership interests were not eligible for like-kind treatment. However, a type of shared ownership is eligible for exchange treatment. The Tenancy in Common is a very special type of group ownership. Any member of the group may dispose of their ownership interest and enter into a 1031 Exchange if they desire.

A tenancy in common is different from a partnership for the following reasons:

1) A legal or defacto partnership is never formed

2) Earnings and expenses are reported as pro rata shares on the individual owner's tax return

3) As a group, owners never request or receive a taxpayer identification number (TIN) from the Internal Revenue Service.

4) A tax return for the group is never filed with the Internal Revenue Service.

5) The deed to the property lists the individual owner(s) as tenants in common.

One of the most common tenancy-in-common real estate practices today is the condominium.

The condo association owns the land, buildings and amenities. The individual owners own the interior space including floor coverings, window treatments, appliances, etc. etc. and an undivided interest in the common elements of the condominium association.

The new Tenancy in Common projects are a very useful tool for those investors wishing to retire from the real estate management business. The investor may have grown tired of leaky faucet phone calls, collecting rents or dealing with the current tenant /landlord laws. A Tenancy in Common ownership in a large office building or 'big box' commercial building could be the relief you have been searching for.

A new use of tenancy in common has become part of the 1031 exchange choices. You can exchange your ownership interest in single family rental properties for a tenancy in common in other investment real property.

A group of owners own the building and hire a management company to manage the building. Typically, there would be 1 to 2 dozen tenants in the building, all under long term leases.

Where do you find this dream ownership? You and a group of friends or business partners can put your own together OR you can look for a company that promotes these projects.

Generally, this is how it works:

A promoter has purchased a $5 Million office building that has 2 tenants. One tenant has 10 years remaining on their underlying lease and two 10-year options to extend. The other tenant has recently moved into the building and has 15 years remaining on its lease and 3 5-year options to renew.

The promoter, who is also a management company, wishes to interest other investors in becoming owners in the building. Gradually, new investors are found. They purchase a percentage of undivided ownership and share in the revenues and expenses for the property to the extent of their ownership share. Normally, the management company will build cash reserves for major repairs or to manage a vacancy period should one of the tenants decide not to renew its lease. These buildings are usually financed with non recourse debt, rents are set at a level which meets all expenses and leaves some profit so the owners receive a return on their investment. Most promoters try to establish a return of 5 to 8% for their investors. Checks are usually issued monthly and sometimes quarterly.

Another excellent use for the Tenant in Common ownership is as a backup for an existing exchange. We all have experienced problems with bringing identified property to contract and closing on it within the allowed 180 days. Sometimes the exchanger becomes so enamored with a specific property; the 45 day identification period passes without their having named an alternative investment. Tenant in Common ownership can be arranged within a few days even in a few hours. But, if it is not identified as a possible replacement property, it cannot be treated as like-kind. Most Qualified Intermediaries have a working relationship with several promoters of Tenant in Common packages and can refer you to them. The choice is yours.

It is important for you to know; as of the printing of this handbook, a secondary market for Tenant-in-Common ownership does not exist. If you invest in a project like this and need to liquidate before the group wants to sell the building, finding a buyer for you undivided interest may not be easy.

What Happens to my Tax Basis in an Exchange?

As mentioned earlier, the tax basis of the property that is relinquished is carried over as the basis of the replacement property. Basis in a capital asset includes several characteristics most people don't even think about. There is your cost basis or what you paid for the property including improvements. There is your tax basis which is your cost basis less any depreciation allowed or allowable on your investment property. There is also the holding period or how long you have owned the property.

There are some adjustments to basis that can be made. For instance, if the replacement property costs more than the sale price of the relinquished property, you may adjust the new basis by the additional cost. The carryover basis retains the same depreciation method used when attached to the Relinquished property. Any additional basis must be assigned current depreciation methods. The basis is also adjusted for the costs of acquisition which are not otherwise deductible. The closing costs could be title insurance, legal fees, search fees, document stamps, transfer taxes, etc.

FOR EXAMPLE:

You contract to sell your relinquished property for $100,000. Your accountant tells you that your tax basis is $42,000. And that $15,000 of the basis is in non-depreciable land. The remaining $27,000 is the book value of the improvement to the land. Your proposed capital gain is $58,000 ($100,000 - $42,000). The property is unencumbered (no mortgage). You have every reason to consider an exchange. The estimated Capital Gain tax is $8,700 without considering the possibility of depreciation recapture.

You locate and identify a property that you negotiate a purchase price of $ 135,000. You elect to acquire a mortgage for the additional money needed to close.

In this example the entire capital gain amount is deferred into the replacement property because you purchased for more than you sold and the mortgage you acquired is not considered taxable boot because you are financing only the increased cost.

Your new tax basis will have several components:

The enhanced Improvements will begin to be depreciated using the depreciation guidelines in effect at the time of closing. In 2005, that would mean MACRS over a 39 (commercial) or 27.5 (residential) year period.

Exchanged Land Value	$15,000.
Exchanged Improvements (Book Value)	27,000.
Depreciation Allowed or Allowable (Not important in this exchange)	19,000.
Enhanced Land Value	7,500.

Enhanced Improvements	27,500.
NEW Basis: Land	$22,500.
Improvements	$54,500.

The land continues to be a non-depreciable asset.

The Exchanged Improvements will continue to be depreciated in the same manner as before. This means that the depreciation rate and years of service remain the same in the new property as in the old property. If the improvements on the new property have a fair market value greater than that of the old property, the difference is depreciated at a new current rate.

What Happens to the Depreciation on My Relinquished Property?

Depreciation is a characteristic of basis and carries over to the replacement property as part of the tax basis. In the previous example we said the $19,000 in depreciation had been allowed over the ownership period of the exchanger. In actuality, we were saying that the exchanger had purchased the property for $61,000 and that $19,000 had been depreciated leaving the current tax basis of $42,000.

When a depreciated property is sold, the gain on the sale has two components; appreciated gain and depreciated gain. Under the current tax code, (2004) depreciated gain, if recapture is required, is taxed at 25% and appreciated gain is taxed at a maximum of 15%.

Proposed Depreciation Schedule:

Relinquished Property

Description	Cost	Date Purchased	Method Life Accum. Deprn
Land	$15,000	Mar 1994	N/A
Improvements	$46,000	Mar 1994	S/L 27.5 yr 19,000

Replacement Property

Description	Cost	Date Purchased	Method Life Accum. Deprn
Land	$15,000	Mar 1994	N/A
Improvements	$46,000	Mar 1994	S/L 27.5 yr 19,000
Land	$7,500	Jun 2005	NA
Improvements	$27,500	Jun 2005	MACRS 39 yr

When a taxpayer enters an exchange and replaces the relinquished property with a property of less value, any difference could be subject to tax, and if it is taxed, it will be at the higher rate first. This means that depreciation gain will be taxed first (depreciation recapture) and appreciation gain will be taxed only when all depreciation gain has been exhausted.

This is true because an asset cannot have a basis that is greater than its fair market value (FMV).

What about my Holding Period on the Relinquished Property?

The holding period is another characteristic of basis. It carries over to the new property along with the substituted basis. In the above example, suppose the exchanger purchased the $61,000 property just 14 years prior to the date he closed on the replacement property. With respect to the $61,000 initial investment in the asset, the 14 years of ownership attached to that portion of the replacement property. As to the enhanced value of the replacement property, the holding period begins anew. The additional $35,000 paid for the new property establishes its own holding period and will be taxed accordingly when disposed of.

If you have held the property you wish to relinquish less that two years, be sure to consult with you tax professional regarding the exchange. There is considerable disagreement regarding exchanges of real property held for less than two years, so make sure your tax preparer understands the exchange process and potential tax consequences.

The Internal Revenue Code and the regulations are silent with regards to how long you must hold the property. However, it is clear that foreigners exchanging personal property are only required to consider the use of the property during their ownership if their ownership is less than two years.

What is Capital Gain?

Capital Gain occurs when you sell a capital asset and realize a profit on the sale. Whether you will be required to recognize the sale as a taxable event will be determined by the circumstances which caused you to convert the asset into cash.

If a government agency (Local, State or Federal) condemned the asset, there are rules which will allow you to replace the asset without having to recognize the sale.

If the asset was destroyed in a natural disaster, there are rules which will allow you to replace the asset without having to recognize the sale.

If the asset was destroyed by a sudden event which was beyond your control (like fire), there are rules which will allow you to replace the asset without having to recognize the sale. Receipt of the insurance proceed constitutes a conversion of the property for cash.

If you elect to sell your primary residence, there are rules which can offer relief from recognition if your entire gain is less than $250,000 ($500,000 if married filing jointly) and you have owned and used the residence as your primary residence for 2 or the 5 years immediately prior to the sale.

Finally, for investors in real estate there is the like-kind exchange which is available. Using the like-kind exchange allows the taxpayer to delay recognition of gain on the sale of a capital asset.

Capital gain can be long-term. This means that you owned the property for a period of time longer than one year. This is where the common phrase, year and a day, is most often heard. Long-term capital gain is currently (2006) taxed at 15%.

Capital gain can also be short term if you owned the property in question for one year or less. Short term capital gain is taxed at whatever the taxpayers prevailing ordinary income rate is for the year of the sale.

FAQ

What if I own real estate as an individual and I wish to include my spouse on title for the replacement property?

The mechanics of the §1031 Exchange require that the title holder be the same at the end of the exchange as at the beginning. In this case, to preserve all of the ability to defer tax on the sale of property, it is recommended that property be purchased having twice the value of that which was relinquished. Essentially the exchanger (you) will exchange 100% interest in the relinquished property for a 50% interest in the replacement property.

Another method, if there is enough time to complete the recording of a deed, would be to put the spouse on the deed of the relinquished property prior to selling the property. This begs the question of how long the spouse must be on title before the exchange begins. The best answer is "longer is better" preferably at least one year and should be done prior to the listing of the property for sale. Unfortunately, some states and local governments will require additional transfer taxes if a new name is added to a deed, so make sure you understand if transfer tax, document stamps or intangible tax will be due.

It is important that the titleholder of the replacement property be the same as the title holder of the relinquished property. If a corporation owns the real estate, then the corporation is the exchanger.

I am a partner in a partnership that owns real estate, can I do an exchange?

Maybe! If you desire to leave the partnership and acquire some real estate in your own name, the answer is NO! An interest in a partnership is not exchangeable for real property. The partnership interest is not like-kind to real property. Under the rules, the partnership interest is not even exchangeable for an interest in another partnership.

However, if the real property owned by the partnership is being sold and the partnership dissolved, you may exchange your undivided interest in the property being sold for other real property to be held for investment purposes.

An example, you along with two buddies formed a partnership and purchased an office building. You have a 1/3 interest in the building. The building is being sold for $600,000. You may reinvest your $200,000 interest in the building in other real property to be held as an investment. Keep in mind that the building may have been mortgaged so you will have to meet the mortgage requirements as well.

If I want to exchange my undivided interest in the partnership real estate, do my partners have to exchange as well?

No, your partners are not required to join you in an exchange. Some or all of your partners may want to do an exchange. You may each use a different intermediary if you choose. If all the partners want to exchange their undivided interest and all the partners are interested in the same property as replacement, it would be best for the partnership to perform the exchange.

Can I exchange a Vacation Rental?

It stands to reason that if you own a vacation rental and meet the personal use rules (the greater of 14 days or 10% of the rental days), that you would be able to exchange a vacation rental. It is clearer if you exchange a vacation rental for a vacation rental but if you follow the rules for investment property, it should not be a problem.

However, when your personal use is greater than the allowed use, you are required to bifurcate or allocate expenses between personal use and investment use. This is usually done on a percentage basis.

There is no authority that addresses such a situation, but it is believed that with an adequate facts and circumstances approach to the exchange, the exchange would survive an audit by the Internal Revenue Service. To determine if you will have a sufficient set of facts and circumstances you should consult you tax preparer or seek competent professional help.

Can I exchange a Guest House?

I own a home which I use as a personal residence. On the same plot of land is a guest house which I have rented every year for the last 15 years. I report my rental income and expenses on Schedule E of my form 1040 and take depreciation on the guest house.

Can I use an exchange for the guest house while claiming primary residence exclusion on the main house?

Again, the Internal Revenue Service requires you to bifurcate or allocate the common expenses of operating the real estate. You must divide the real estate taxes and other expenses between the two dwelling units.

While there is no authority that addresses this specific situation, it is reasonable that when a facts and circumstances test is applied, the same ratio of basis allotted to the guest house over the 15 year period could be applied to the Fair Market Value of the real estate at the time of sale. In this way a value for the investment property could be established and adequate arguments could be presented that support the guest house portion of the property being eligible for §1031 exchange treatment.

Again, it is important that you seek competent professional advice in any situation that is not clear cut.

Why isn't my second home considered an investment? I bought it so I would receive the appreciated value when I sold.

Webster's dictionary defines an investment as the outlay of money usually for income or profit. Interestingly enough, if you purchased the house and left it vacant, it would probably qualify as investment property. However, capital assets that are used personally and exclusively by the owner do not qualify for non recognition treatment under §1031. There is no 'tax haven' for the 'Second Home'. You can create one by converting its use to investment. This can be accomplished by renting the property for a period of time and most of all STOP USING IT PERSONALLY.

I understand the related party rules as they affect 1031 exchanges, but what if the related party dies?

If either party to a related party exchange dies during the 24 month period immediately following the last transaction in the exchange the non-recognition clause will not apply.

This means that the exchange will remain intact and the gain continues to be deferred.

The same will apply if either the relinquished or the replacement property is converted to cash through a compulsory or involuntary conversion. Such a conversion will occur if a government takes the property by imminent domain proceedings or if the property is destroyed by fire, flood, or other natural disaster.

Can I exchange three properties for only one property? How would it work?

It is perfectly reasonable to exchange three properties for a single property. It is a little more work and the intermediary may charge for the extra work, especially if the relinquished properties are sold to three different purchasers and represent three entirely separate closings.

The time lines are the same; 180 days for the entire exchange period and 45 days for the identification period. Both periods begin as of the closing of the first property. All property, relinquished and replacement, must be identified within the 45 days period so make sure you have 1031 language in any contract signed during the identification period or that you have properly identified the property to your intermediary.

As to the basis in the new property, it will be the aggregate of the bases of the three properties. Depreciation methods and length of holding period will remain the same as it was with each of the relinquished properties. This can be a bit of a problem and inexpensive fixed asset software should be able to handle it. Of course, if the replacement property costs more than the aggregate of the relinquished properties' sale prices, a fourth depreciation factor will have to be figured into the process.

What about exchanging one property for three properties?

Again, the process remains the same as far as time constraints are concerned. How the basis in the relinquished property is treated is a little different. In this case, the aggregate value of the replacement properties would be compared to the selling price of the relinquished property and ratios developed.

Each of the replacement properties would assume its proportionate share of the basis. Again depreciation method and length of time remain the same. Any additional price paid for a replacement property would be added to basis but depreciated using acceptable depreciation methods in effect at the time of the purchase.

I own two unimproved (vacant) lots. Can I sell one and use the proceeds to build a rental unit on the other as part of a §1031 exchange?

This is one area that investors would love to see a change in the regulations. You won't find the answer in §1031 of the code but you will find the answer in §1033 regarding condemnations and the deferral of taxes.

The regulations require that "dirt" be exchanged for "dirt". If you sell land and replace it with a dwelling unit on another lot you already own, you have not met the "dirt for dirt" criteria and the replacement property will not be considered like-kind to the relinquished property.

There are some recent Private Letter Rulings (PLRs) issued by the Internal Revenue Service that could make this possible through the use of long term leases (greater than 30 years). The legal gymnastics required are generally cost prohibitive except in the case of large land holdings which are being developed into industrial parks.

Can I sign a contract to purchase my replacement property before my relinquished property sells?

Absolutely!! The time lines set out in the regulations are always as of the closing date of the first transaction in an exchange. There is nothing that prohibits you from contracting the replacement property earlier than the transfer or closing on the relinquished property.

BE CAREFUL that your closing date is sufficiently far enough in the future so you are not forced into a reverse exchange. There is nothing wrong with a reverse exchange, they are merely more expensive and many lenders will withdraw their commitment when they hear you want to deed the property to a third party. A little attention to this detail can avoid those added costs and frustrations.

My buyer is having trouble finding a lender; can I take back a note on my relinquished property?

The regulations indicate that a security agreement such as a mortgage or a deed of trust is one of the 'safe harbors' from constructive receipt of the proceeds.

However, if you elect to take back a note, make sure it is secured with a mortgage and/or Deed of Trust and that the note cannot be construed as cash or a cash equivalent. It is important that no payments on the note be received by you during the exchange period. Payments can be made in advance at closing or monthly payments can be sent to the intermediary until the exchange is complete.

In making a decision to finance the sale or a part of it, rely on the advice of your attorney or tax preparer. You will want to adequately protect your interest in the property.

I have often heard that a leasehold interest of 30 years or more was equivalent to ownership in fee. Do leaseholds of 30 years or more qualify for like-kind exchange treatment?

Yes, it does. In fact, if you hold a leasehold interest in increments of 30 years, say like a 99 year lease with 92 years remaining, you may exchange the next 30 year period and regain possession of the leasehold in the 31st year.

How much money must I reinvest?

There are very few cases where only the proceeds need to be reinvested. The regulations require that the exchanger's economic condition cannot be improved by the exchange. Therefore, reinvesting only the proceeds from the sale may not meet the criteria for a complete deferral.

In order to accomplish this, the fair market value of the replacement property should be equal to or greater than that of the relinquished property. Your equity in the replacement property should be the same as or greater than your equity in the relinquished property. If you had a mortgage on the relinquished property it is usually best to have a mortgage of the same or greater value on the replacement property as well.

Can I get money out of the exchange to use for other purposes?

Generally no! The proceeds of the sale of the relinquished property go to the intermediary and the intermediary uses those funds to purchase the replacement property. You may have to procure a mortgage in order to provide all the money necessary to close on the replacement property.

During the exchange period,
you may not have access
to the proceeds at any time.

However, it is possible for you to take money out before the exchange begins or after it ends. You can chose to equity finance prior to selling or better yet, before you list the relinquished property for sale or you can refinance the mortgage at some point after closing on the replacement property. There is at least one instance where the exchanger borrowed against the relinquished property prior to closing the sale and the IRS was successful in challenging their receipt of cash money. The money was declared boot and tax was due.

Some tax professionals may encourage you to take a larger mortgage than necessary on the replacement property. This will allow the exchanger to receive the excess money at closing. When you do this, the excess funds may be returned to you at closing by the closing agent or the intermediary may send less money to closing and write you a check at the end of the exchange. Either way, the cash you get will be taxable boot. Normally, borrowed money is not subject to tax, but when using an exchange any excess borrowing causes your economic condition to change and you have received cash boot. This can be a dangerous method for taking money out of the exchange. The primary reason is that mortgages must be balanced to make sure you have not received mortgage boot.

You must always keep in mind, the Internal Revenue Service wants to tax whatever amounts it can and it will be you that must defend your method. Often, the cost of defense is greater than the tax on the amount received. The author's opinion is: Do not tempt the IRS. Take some equity financing on the relinquished or equity finance the replacement or if you choose, refinance the mortgage on the replacement.

The important thing to remember is to understand the rules so you can make informed decisions.

What happens if I receive some of the proceeds from closing on the Relinquished property?

This could be a fatal flaw for the exchange. If the closing agent draws a check payable to you for a portion of the proceeds, this would be an indication that you have dominion and control over the proceeds. After all, the closing agent must have taken direction from you and followed it. While there is no certainty to the outcome, it is safe to say that the IRS would probably construe your receipt of funds as constructive receipt of the proceeds and your exchange will be declared a sale and purchase. Tax will be due. See the Florida Industries v. Commissioner in the Appendix entitled Court Cases.

How far in advance of the sale of the relinquished property, can I refinance if I need to?

There is no time period than can be considered absolutely safe or absolutely a problem. There is at least one court case where the IRS pursued the exchanger because of refinancing prior to closing on the relinquished property. In that instance, the Court looked at the purpose for the refinance and how the funds were used. Since the funds were used for real estate investment purposes, the Court found in favor of the exchanger. Using the borrowed funds to pay for personal items like a new car or your daughter's wedding might draw a different conclusion.

It is my opinion that any refinancing of the relinquished property should occur prior to the listing of the property for sale. Even then, be prepared to defend your position if necessary.

In the case of refinancing the replacement property, longer is better. Wait as long as you can before refinancing. Again the purpose for the additional borrowing may play an important part in defending your action.

Can I use the proceeds to make deposits on the replacement property?

Yes, the funds held by the intermediary can be used to make the good faith deposit as well as additional deposits on the replacement property.

Checks should not be made payable to you but to the escrow agent holding the deposits on the contract. That escrow agent should not be your attorney.

The contract to purchase should stipulate when additional deposits are due. In the case of an additional deposit required in order to extend the closing date on the contract, make sure an addendum is prepared showing the required deposit and the new closing date. This is important because you have assigned the contract to your intermediary. The intermediary can only follow the terms of the contract.

If I make the good faith deposit from my personal funds, can I be reimbursed?

Technically the answer is yes. It is best to recover these funds at the end of the exchange if there is money left over. If it is necessary that you be reimbursed immediately, make sure the intermediary has a copy of the contract requiring the deposit and a copy of the check showing it was drawn on your personal funds. If your deposit was made by way of a promissory note due at closing, it is not reimbursable.

How do I report the exchange on my tax return?

For the tax year in which the exchange began, form 8824 (Like-Kind Exchanges) must be included in you tax return.

It is very important that you never file a tax return for the year in which the exchange began until the exchange is completed or the exchange period has expired.

The Courts have held on several occasions that tax returns filed when an exchange is incomplete effectively ends the exchange period. Property received after the date the tax return is filed will not be considered like-kind to the relinquished property.

If your exchange is not completed by April 15 of the year following the beginning of the exchange period, simply file an automatic extension of time to file. Make sure any taxes that might be due with the extension are timely paid so the extension is valid.

How long must I have owned the property I wish to relinquish?

Section 1031 offers little guidance when searching for an answer to this question. If we look to Section 1221 which describes what a Capital Asset is, we will find information that will tell you the holding period of the relinquished asset is tacked on to the holding period of the replacement property.

This means that if you have owned the relinquished property for 5 years and dispose of it in a §1031 exchange the replacement property will assume all of the characteristics of basis from the relinquished property. This includes holding period. Therefore, you will have owned the replacement property (or some portion of it) for 5 years at the time you close on the property.

Currently, there are differences in opinion among Qualified Intermediaries, Accommodators and tax preparers. Obviously, the longer you hold the property the better.

It is necessary that you have held the property long enough and in a manner consistent with investment use that the IRS will be unable to claim that you held the property for resale. Holding property for resale would indicate the property was inventory and remember from earlier on in this handbook, inventory does not qualify for like-kind exchange.

How long must I hold the replacement property?

The answer to this question is as difficult as the last. You should plan to hold the property as long as necessary to show that your intent to enter into an exchange was bonafide. However, there are instances when you have become the new owner of property that someone else wants at any price.

If this should happen, make sure you have not made any indication to anyone that the property is for sale. Do not discuss selling the property with Realtors or even family members.

The offer you receive from the person willing to pay anything to have that piece of property must be unsolicited. In fact, if you accept the offer make sure you get a notarized letter from the buyer that his offer was unsolicited and that he approached you about selling.

There are never any promises that your word will be accepted at face value by the IRS. Always document and the more documentation the better off you will be.

Finally, as with the relinquished property, the length of time the property is held and its use must be consistent with investment use.

If you have purchased your replacement property from a related person, be very careful that you hold the property a minimum of 24 calendar months and that you and your relative file form 8824 for two years following the year of the exchange. An unsolicited offer to sell will probably not work for you. This means that your property is not eligible for exchange into another property for the 24 month period.

Suppose I have a second home and wish to exchange it?

Second homes which are used personally are not eligible for like-kind treatment. However, you can change the use of the property and thereby make it eligible. You can do that by making it clear to colleagues and family members that you no longer intend to use the property for personal use. Follow up on that by contacting a Real Estate Rental Management company and list the property for rent. The rents requested should be fair market value. There should be nothing in the offer to lease that would discourage a potential renter. Whether you offer the property for annual lease or seasonal lease does not really matter. **Any fair market value renter is better than none. But please, the one thing you must included in your plan, do not use the property personally.**

How long should I hold the property after I convert its use?

There is no firm period of time to guide you. Only, "longer is better". Make sure you rely on your tax preparer for the best advice for your situation. And, document, document, document. There is no such thing as too much documentation when changing from personal use to investment use.

There is case law (see appendix) that suggests the holding period of converted personal use real estate could be as little as a few months.

Can I exchange investment property and later convert it to personal use (primary residence) property?

Indeed you can. This seems to be a favorite tool for retirement planning. Most guidelines will indicate that you should continue the investment use for a minimum of two years especially if your plan is to convert its use to personal use.

As with other questions regarding changing the use of property, the longer you maintain the investment use the better your chances of the exchange surviving an audit by the IRS.

There is always the requirement that the taxpayer enter an exchange with the bonafide intent to complete the exchange. Unforeseen changes in circumstances can alter the eventual outcome but do not necessarily change your intent.

I engaged an intermediary to facilitate an exchange. Now I have decided not to do it. What will happen now?

That will depend on what stage of the exchange you are in.

If you have not yet closed on the relinquished property, simply notify the intermediary that you do not wish to proceed. Depending on how much work the intermediary has done, there may be a cancellation fee.

If you have closed on the relinquished property and the intermediary has received the proceeds but you have not identified any replacement property then you should notify the intermediary that you do not wish to proceed. Since you have not identified any replacement property, your exchange will end on the 46th day of the exchange period and the proceeds will be sent to you at that time.

However, if you have identified replacement property and you are still in the identification period you can simply notify the intermediary, issue a written revocation of you identification and your exchange will end on the 46th day.

If the above circumstance applies to you and you are beyond the identification period, you should still notify your intermediary that you do not intend to close on any of the identified property. Unfortunately, your exchange period will have to expire (180 days) before the proceeds will be forwarded to you.

If I own property I acquired by way of an exchange, can I exchange it for another property?

Yes, it would be a new exchange and the basis carried over from the originally relinquished property would be substituted into your new replacement property plus any adjustments.

How often can I exchange properties I acquire by way of an exchange?

This is tricky because you don't want to exchange so often that it appears you are flipping property. Flipping property makes the property look more like inventory and inventory is not eligible for exchange treatment. There is no fixed number of times you can exchange and depending on the circumstances there is not fixed time period you must meet. Always, holding the property for investment is the intent and "longer is better." Consult with your tax adviser about this.

What happens if I am unable to identify property I wish to acquire?

Without a proper identification you exchange will end on the 46th day. The disposal of the relinquished property will be treated as a sale and tax will be due if you have capital gain.

What if I cannot close on identified property?

Once the identification period has ended you may only acquire identified property and have it considered like-kind to your relinquished property. If you are unable to close on any of the identified property, the exchange period will end and on the 181st day, the proceeds will be sent to you. The disposal of the relinquished property will be treated as a sale.

When I identify property, how specific do I have to be?

You must be very specific and unambiguous. The absolute best ID is to use the Tax I.D. number assigned by the tax assessor's office. Second best and also sufficient is to use the complete mailing address for the property. If the property does not have a mailing address, then you should use the legal description included in the deed held by the current owner.

The property I wish to acquire needs repairs. Can the repairs be included in the exchange?

It is best to have the seller of the property make necessary repairs and increase the price of the property accordingly. Minor repairs are often included at settlement and the closing agent escrows funds to make sure the repairs are completed. This can work if the repairs are minor and not material. However, if the repairs are such that they are major repairs or even renovations, then it is best to acquire the property in a reverse exchange with the accommodator holding title to the property. Repairs will be made while the accommodator holds title and will be included in the Fair Market Value when the accommodator deeds the property to you. Your tax professional can help you determine if the needed repairs are material or not.

I am having a dwelling built on a lot owned by the builder. What will happen if the improvement is not finished by the 180th day?

This is probably one of the major reasons exchanges fail. You must take ownership of the property before the end of exchange period. Most builders will not transfer property before construction is completed.

Some things you can do to avoid this problem:

Contract for the new construction before the relinquished property is sold. Coordinate the closing of the relinquished property with the completion of the replacement property.

Consider a reverse exchange. Even though it is more expensive, it is better than losing the exchange benefits completely.

Consider purchasing a model home and leasing it back to the builder.

I want to purchase a vacant lot and have a dwelling constructed. It won't be ready in 180 days. How will that work?

This can be handled in one of two ways. It can be a reverse exchange where the accommodator takes title to the lot and causes the dwelling to be constructed using funds provided by you.

If the construction can be nearly completed within the 180 days allowed and you don't need 100% completion to meet the exchange requirements, you can receive the benefit of the percentage completed.

This is accomplished by having an appraiser/engineer estimate the percent of the construction that is complete as of the 179th day. The property will transfer to you on the 180th day and you will be credited with the percent that is complete. An example: The completed structure is contracted to cost $400,000 and is estimated to be 75% complete. Your exchange credit will be the cost of the lot plus $300,000 (75% of $400,000).

See the next section for the other method....

I want to build on a vacant lot and the construction will take more than a year including permitting and environmental. How can this be done?

This is easier and less risky than having to complete construction within the 180 day time frame. You should enter into an agreement with an accommodator or a builder for a 'build to suit' arrangement. If you chose an accommodator, it should go like this: The accommodator will set up a separate entity (Corporation or LLC) to hold title to the vacant lot. The titleholder will have to show all of the indices of ownership; pay the taxes, pay the insurance, sign the contract with the construction company, make the construction draws – all the things you would have to due if you purchased the lot and initiated construction. You will lend the construction money to the titleholder. When the property is within 6 months of being complete, you will sell your relinquished property and the proceeds will go to an intermediary. Later when the construction is complete, you will actually purchase the property from the titleholder in a fully documented title transfer with all required transfer taxes and recording fees paid at closing.

This scenario can take as long as it takes to acquire the land, permit it and complete the construction.

I don't want to purchase property for the same value as what I sell. What will be the repercussions?

Any time you buy for less than you sell, there may to tax due. How much tax will be due depends on your costs of sale and purchase. Not all closing costs are included in the calculation. Sales commission is always included but be sure to meet with your tax professional to determine the exact effect in your situation.

I am a foreign person who owns US real estate. Do I qualify for a §1031 exchange?

Yes, you do so long as you are willing to reinvest in property located in the United States or its possessions. In addition, the property cannot be a second home. You will still have to meet the FIRPTA requirements for withholding. Foreign nationals who use §1031 are exempted from paying tax on the sale but the paperwork must be filed and a non-recognition certificate received.

The gain on my primary residence is substantially more than the exclusion allows. Can I exchange the property?

You can, after you convert its use to investment. Remember, §1031 is not an exclusion. It is only a deferral. You will be giving up your claim to the exclusion if you convert its use and later exchange it for other investment property.

I want to roll all my investment properties to the area I am retiring to. Is there a limit on how many exchanges you can do?

There is no limit to how many exchanges you can do. Actually you can do them all in a single exchange (dangerous) or you can take your time and do them one at a time. A lot less stressful!

If I use a §1031 exchange to acquire property in the region where I wish to retire, can I later move into it?

Yes, you can move into it and convert its use from investment to primary residence. However, it is generally recognized that you should continue the investment use for at least 24 months after acquiring the property in a 1031 exchange.

Can I later sell the property and take the primary residence exclusion?

The IRS has recently issued new guidelines on the sale of a primary residence which was acquired by way of a 1031 exchange. The sale and the exclusion is not prohibited but instead of the 2 of 5 year rule which applies to primary residences which were purchased for that reason. The primary residence which was acquired by way of a 1031 exchange will have to be owned at least the 5 full years before the exclusion will be allowed. So, you can rent it for 24 months and move into it. Live in it a minimum of 3 years and then sell. The primary residence exclusion ($250,000 per MFJ taxpayer) will be allowed. The only consideration you need to be concerned with is whether there is depreciation recapture required on any of the depreciation that is part of your basis.

I own a condo which I rent out. I want to exchange it for a vacant lot. I know I can do it but are there any pitfalls?

The only concern I am aware of is depreciation. A vacant lot is a non-depreciable asset. Some tax preparers believe that depreciation cannot be part of the basis which is substituted into the lot. So, check with you tax preparer on whether you can park the depreciation or whether you should recapture it.

Worksheets

Basis Substitution

Begin with:
Relinquished Prop #1: Basis #1
Relinquished Prop #2: Basis #2
Relinquished Prop #3: <u>Basis #3</u>
Total   Sum Basis

To determine how much of the basis goes to each of the replacement properties, do this:

Replacement Prop #1: GPP #1
Replacement Prop #2: <u>GPP #2</u>
Total   Sum GPP

Then:

GPP #1 / Sum GPP = Ratio #1
GPP #2 / Sum GPP = Ratio #2

Where GPP = Gross Purchase Price. GPP is the contract price plus costs of closing the purchase. Prepaid items and recurring expenses such as real estate tax or condo fees are excluded from this calculation.

Then:
Relin #1 X Ratio #1 = Share of basis
Relin #2 X Ratio #1 = Share of basis
Relin #3 X Ratio #1 = <u>Share of basis</u>
Total   Transferred Basis
                   For Repl #1

Do the same for each replacement property using its respective ratio.

Each share of basis from the relinquished property(s) continues to be depreciated in the same manner and life as was occurring in its respective relinquished property.

This means; if you were depreciating using straight line for 30 years and there are 20 years to go you continue to depreciate this portion at straight line for the next 20 years.

Likewise Acrs and Macrs depreciation methods would continue for whatever remaining life was in the substituted share of the basis.

Do not forget to transfer the land basis as well. The character of the land as a non depreciable asset and its value remains the same.

Additional Basis if You Bought Up

To determine if you have basis in addition to that which was substituted from the relinquished property(s), apply the following:

> Relin Prop#1NSP
> Relin Prop#2NSP
> Relin Prop#3NSP
> Total   Sum NSP

NSP equals Net Selling Price. NSP is the contract price less costs of selling the property as shown on settlement sheet. Real Estate taxes and other recurring costs and prepaid items are excluded from this calculation.

Determine the GPP (Gross Purchase Price) for the replacement properties. This was originally calculated in the basis substitution worksheet.

Then:

Sum GPP - Sum NSP = Additional Basis

If you have additional basis, you must first look at the non depreciable land values substituted from the relinquished properties. If the sum of the land value is too low, you must use some or the entire additional basis for new land value.

Any additional basis remaining after adjusting land values may be depreciated according to current depreciation methods.

Appendix A

Property that <u>Does Not Qualify</u>
For Like-Kind Treatment

Foreign Real Estate is not like-kind to United States Real Estate.

Primary Residences are not like-kind to single Family Rental property or any other type of rental property.

Second Homes are not like-kind to Single Family Rental property or to Rental Condo property or to any other type of investment property.

Personal use property (Primary residence or second home) is not like-kind to investment property.

Gold Coins are not like-kind to bullion or to bullion quality coins.

Land (vacant or not) is not like-kind to an improvement on another parcel of land already owned by the taxpayer.

Appendix B

Property that <u>Does Qualify</u> for Like-Kind Treatment

A rental single family residence is like-kind to a duplex or a quadruplex.

A rental condominium is like-kind to a rental single family residence.

A rental dwelling unit is like-kind to a commercial rental unit.

A vacant lot or land is like-kind to investment rental real estate.

A farm used for income production is like-kind to other investment property. Exclude the farm house if used as primary residence of owner.

Appendix C

§1031 Checklist of To-Dos

To defer all Capital Gain and Depreciation Recapture tax, the following MUST be met:

1) Engage one or more of the 'Safe Harbors' allowed by the IRS
   Qualified Intermediary
   Qualified Escrow Accounts
   Qualified Trust
   Security or Guarantee Arrangement
   Mortgage, Deed of Trust, or other security interest in property so long as it is not cash or cash equivalents.

2) Enter into a process that clearly shows your intention to engage in the exchange.

3) Identify your replacement property within 45 days of the closing date of your relinquished property.

4) Take ownership of the replacement property within 180 days of the closing date of your relinquished property.

5) Make sure the value of the property acquired is greater than or equal to the value of the property relinquished with some very limited adjustments.

6) The value of a mortgage you are relieved of at the transfer of the relinquished property must be replaced with a mortgage of equal or greater value on the replacement property. Be careful about taking too large a mortgage. It may put cash in you pocket and become taxable boot.

7) Do not file a tax return for the year in which the exchange period began until after the exchange is completed or the exchange period has ended. Doing so will end the exchange period.

Remember to get professional help!!

Glossary

§1031 Exchange
A method for exchanging property whereby the exchanger can defer all capital gain taxes if certain rules are met.

Accommodator
In a reverse exchange the Accommodator serves as the unrelated third party that accomplishes the exchange in behalf of the exchanger.

Assignment
A party to a contract gives their contractual rights to another party.

Basis
The portion of a capital asset an owner has not yet recovered by way of depreciation.

Boot
Cash or mortgage that does not qualify for like-kind treatment in a 1031 exchange.

Build to Suit
A method that can be used to stretch the construction period beyond the 180 exchange period by timing the transfer of the relinquished property to within 180 days of the completion of the specified replacement property.

Capital Gain
The portion of an owners equity that results from appreciated value.

Exchange Period
The 180 day period following the first transaction in the exchange process.

Exchange First
In a reverse exchange, the property to be purchased is identified as replacement property and acquired by the exchanger. The relinquished property is parked with the EAT.

Exchange Last
In a Reverse Exchange, the replacement property is held by the accommodator's EAT. The identification of the Relinquished property can be delayed until after the replacement property is acquired

Forward Exchange
The relinquished property sale transaction occurs first.

Identification Period
The period within the exchange period that is the first 45 days after the first transaction takes place.

Like-Kind
Refers to properties that are held for investment or used in a trade or business in the hands of the owner.

LLC (Limited Liability Company)
A legal entity that can own property and perform services very much like a corporation but whose participants are members rather than shareholders.

Mortgage
An encumbrance on real property that secures a lender's interest in a promissory note.

Parking Transaction
A reverse exchange is commonly referred to as a parking transaction because the replacement property is parked in the name of an Exchange Accommodation Titleholder and transferred to the exchanger at a later date.

Phantom Income
Income that is not realized by the taxpayer but becomes taxable. The most common is interest income imputed on Original Issue Discount transactions.

Qualified Intermediary
The person or entity that is not disqualified from serving as a qualified intermediary who sells and purchases the exchange properties for the exchanger.

Relinquished Property
The property being disposed of by the exchanger.

Replacement Property
The property being acquired by the exchanger.

Reverse Exchange
A process whereby the exchanger acquires the replacement property first through an Exchange Accommodation Titleholder.

Safe Harbor
Processes offered within the IRS regulations that are considered safe and will not be questioned by the IRS when followed.

Starker
The family who in the 1960's successfully challenged the exchange rules and completed the first successful delayed exchange.

Tax Basis
The unrecovered cost of an asset. Generally this is cost plus improvements and less depreciation allowed or allowable.

White Knight
This party comes to the rescue of an exchanger whose forward exchange has gone sour and is forced to close on the replacement property before the relinquished transaction is completed. A white knight can also rescue the Reverse Exchange.

Alphabet Soup

EAT- Exchange Accommodation Titleholder

IRC - Internal Revenue Code. Laws passed by Congress regarding the taxation of persons and the regulations which interpret the law.

IRS - Internal Revenue Service. An agency of the Treasury Department charged with the implementation of tax law and the collection of taxes.

OID - Original Issue Discount. Interest imputed on the face value of a delayed negotiable instrument.

PLR - Private Letter Ruling requested by a taxpayer and issued by the IRS.

QEAA- Qualified Exchange Accommodation Agreement

QI - Qualified Intermediary

QIO - Qualified Indicia of Ownership - Those Burdens and Benefits of ownership that clearly indicate the owner of property.

TAM - Technical Advice Memorandum issued by the IRS

Case Studies

GO FIGURE

John Spencer's Calculated Decisions
A Case Study - or two

Getting the information
Acting on it

Case Study I   Forward Exchange

How to calculate your tax basis?

John Spencer purchased rental property in 1993 for which he paid $75,000.00 - John made renovations in 1995 totaling $4,500.00. All other changes to the property have been handled as repairs.

PURCHASE PRICE	$75,000.00
+ RENOVATIONS	$ 4,500.00
TOTAL COST	**$79,500.00**
- DEPRECIATION TAKEN	$21,373.20
TAX BASIS	**$58,126.80**

The tax rate on Capital Gain is determined by how long the taxpayer has held the property/investment.

Short Term < 1 Years	Your tax Bracket
Long Term > 1 Years	15%

John Spencer discovered that if he sells his rental property he will have to pay 15% of his profit of $58,126.80 ($11,625.36) as a Capital Gain Tax.

How to calculate your Capital Gain?

John Spencer decided to sell the rental property he had purchased in 1993. Using the information developed when he determined his tax basis, the following is an estimate of the Capital Gain John would recognize.

SELLING PRICE	$200,000
COST OF SALE:	
- COMMISSIONS	$ 12,000
- CLOSING	$ 3,000
NET SELLING PRICE	$185,000
LESS THE TAX BASIS	$ 58,126
CAPITAL GAIN	$126,874

How to estimate the tax due?

John Spencer now knows how much Capital Gain he should receive. The next step in determining if an exchange is reasonable is to compute the estimated tax due if he were to sell the property.

The Capital Gain he calculated is:

$126,874

THE GAIN HAS TWO COMPONENTS:

I.	**DEPRECIATION RECAPTURE**	$ 21,374
II.	LONG TERM CAPITAL	$105,500

	CALCULATED CAPITAL GAIN	$126,874

Depreciation is recaptured and taxed at 25%. In John's case this is $5,343.50

Long Term Capital Gain is currently taxed at 15%, in John's case this amount is $15,825.

TOTAL ESTIMATED TAX DUE
$21,168.50
(IF THE PROPERTY IS SOLD)

Should John Spencer enter into a Like–Kind Exchange?

Yes, John should seriously consider a 1031 exchange.

<u>For Comparison</u>

An exchange of property in a case similar to John Spencer's would incur exchange fees in the neighborhood of $1,000 – $1,500.

This exchange will produce a reinvestment opportunity of approximately $20,000 otherwise lost to capital gain taxes.

COST OF AN EXCHANGE

Forward 1031 Exchange	$1,000 - $1500.
Sale and Purchase	$20,000 of **LOST** Investment Opportunity

Case Study II

Reverse Exchange

John Spencer's Real Estate Agent has found the perfect property for John to add to his investment portfolio. But, John needs time to sell the property he wants to relinquish. The price is right and it won't be on the market long. This property is just what John has been looking for to move his retirement plans forward. What can John do?

A reverse exchange? Yes! That's what John should consider and it's what his Realtor® should suggest.

This property is a large home that has been divided into three separate apartment units. It needs some renovations before it can produce rent. The property can be purchased for $200,000.

The property John intends to relinquish (sell) in the exchange is valued at $400,000.

John Spencer's calculations will be done in the same way as the forward exchange in Case I.

John needs to determine if this exchange, as presented, will be beneficial.

Calculating Basis in Replacement Property

PURCHASE PRICE REPLACEMENT	$250,000
NET SELLING PRICE RELINQUISHED	$185,000

DIFFERENCE	$ 65,000 POTENTIAL TAX DUE IF NEGATIVE
TAX BASIS IN RELINQUISHED	$ 58,126
NEW TAX BASIS	$123,126
CAPITAL GAIN TRAPPED IN NEW PROPERTY	$126,874

The Next Decision

If John Spencer decides that it is in his best interest to do a reverse exchange one more decision is required. Should he:

Exchange First

John can <u>exchange first</u> by deeding his current property to an intermediary/accommodator **before** purchasing the new property.

- Or -

Exchange Last

John can <u>exchange last</u> by lending his accommodator the funds necessary to purchase the new property. The property would be titled in the name of the accommodator until the relinquished property is sold. The decision John makes here is determined by the circumstances surrounding the transaction. These circumstances are discussed in the chapter on reverse exchanges.

Case Study III - The Combo Exchange

John Spencer has several properties he wants to exchange for a property he intends to use for retirement in a few years. He has several properties to relinquish and only wants to acquire the one replacement property. The problem – he doesn't think he can contract and close on all the relinquished properties before he has to acquire the replacement property. The properties to be sold have different expirations on their leases. One of them he is sure the tenant wants to purchase. The others he has to move the tenants out clean up the property and list it for sale. He thinks they will sell quickly once on the market.

Here is how the combo exchange can help John. He should begin looking for his replacement property and checking with real estate management companies about getting the property rented. He will have to hold the property as investment for at least 24 months. At the same time he needs to examine the leases on the relinquished properties and determine when each lease ends and map out his strategy.

The combo exchange is actually two exchanges. A forward exchange and a Reverse exchange. Between the two exchanges as much as 360 days of exchange period can be utilized.

Here's the mechanics of it:

John gets his relinquished properties ready for sale. At the same time he finds his replacement property. Two of his relinquished properties will close within

60 days. John is negotiating with the owner of the property he wants to acquire. The owner wants to use the property one last winter season and sets the closing for 6 months away.

John closes on the two relinquished properties using an intermediary. He continues to ready his other properties for sale. On the 45th day of his exchange period, he meets with his intermediary, he has sold and closed on two of the properties, another is expected to close before the replacement property closes.

The aggregate value of the three relinquished properties is 56% of the value of the replacement property. John identifies the three properties to be disposed of and included in the forward part of the exchange and he identifies that the exchange equity from these properties will be used to acquire 56% of the replacement property. The replacement property is due to close in 2½ months.

Prior to closing on the replacement property, the intermediary initiates accommodation documents for the balance (44%) of the replacement property.

The two remaining relinquished properties are identified in the accommodation agreement as the property to be sold and 44% of the replacement property is identified as that which is to be acquired.

At closing, John takes title to 56% of the property and the Accommodator's EAT takes title to the remaining 44%. They own the property as tenants in common.

John must take title to the 56% in order to close out the forward exchange. He does not want to have title to the remaining 44% because he still owns the two properties to be relinquished.

John probably could deed the two remaining relinquished properties to the accommodator and take title to 100% of the replacement property. It is absolutely crucial that the accommodation agreement spell out how the exchange is to be accomplished.

Once the replacement property is closed, John now has another 180 days to sell and close on the two remaining relinquished properties.

Pretty slick!

Court Cases
&
Precedents

And the Courts Say.........

Case #1

Bundren v. Commissioner,
KTC 2002-97 (10th Cir. 2002)

Summary

The taxpayer had a primary residence which they purchased in 1982 for $183,000 and in the next 10 years made $50,000 in improvements. Therefore, their basis in their primary residence was $223,000. In June of 1994 the taxpayers converted their primary residence into rental property.

In September, 1994, they listed the property for sale for $134,500. In December 1994, they exchanged the property for another investment property. The exchange credit was based on the listed sale price.

The IRS challenged the depreciation deduction on the exchanged property as excessive and the loss claimed on the taxpayers 1996 tax return; the year they sold the exchanged property. The taxpayers and the IRS agreed that the exchange transaction qualified under 26 U.S.C. Section 1031 and that "boot" had been received. The only remaining issue was the carryover basis of the converted primary residence to the exchange property.

The Court agreed with the IRS because.....

The basis in property as described in the IRS Code and the regulations are always the lower of cost or Fair Market Value. The question to be answered is what the fair market value was on the date of conversion. Since the taxpayer listed the property for $134,500 and exchanged it at that value only six months after the conversion, the commissioner (of the IRS) determined that $134,500 was its Fair Market Value on the date of conversion and that the more than $200,000 depreciable basis which was used as the basis in the exchange property was excessive and disallowed the excessive depreciation and the excessive loss reported on the taxpayers tax returns.

Interesting points in this case.....

You can convert your primary residence to rental property

The IRS appeared to be unconcerned about the short holding period as investment property. You may not have to hold the converted investment property for 24 months prior to an exchange

The basis in the converted investment property is your cost or its fair market value on the date of conversion whichever is lower.

Lesson in this case.....

The IRS can and will reach back to examine your carryover basis.

Case #2

Christensen v. Commissioner,
KTC 1999-535 (9th Cir. 1998)

Summary

The taxpayers entered into an exchange in late 1988. Their 1988 tax return was due on April 15, 1989. The taxpayers did not acquire their replacement property prior to the due date of their tax return, failed to request an extension of the April 15 filing dead line, furthermore, they filed a tax return that did not include information regarding the exchange.

The IRS challenged the non-recognition of gain on the exchanged property. The commissioner determined that the transfer of properties did not qualify for like-kind treatment.

The Court agreed with the IRS because......

Code section 1031(a) (3) (B) (ii) clearly sets the time limit for completing an exchange as 180 days from the first transfer of property or the due date plus granted extensions of the taxpayers tax return for the year in which the exchange *began*. The taxpayers filed their 1988 tax return which effectively ended their exchange period. Property received after the exchange period has ended cannot be considered of a like-kind.

Interesting points in this case.......

If your exchange period extends beyond the due date of the tax return for the year in which the exchange began, request an automatic extension of time to file. The automatic extension will reset your due date as August 15 allowing more than enough time to complete any exchange that began prior to January 1.

Lesson in this case.......

Do not file your tax return for the year in which the exchange began until the exchange is complete and you can report the entire transaction.

Case #3

DeCleene v. Commissioner,
115 T.C. 457

Summary

Taxpayer operated his business on property (property A) he owned since 1977. In 1992, the taxpayer purchased an unimproved lot (property B) at another location. In September, 1993, the taxpayer entered into an agreement with another party (X) wherein they agreed that the improved property A was of equal value to the unimproved lot, property B. The taxpayer quit claimed property B to taxpayer X for a deferred cash consideration of $142,000.

Taxpayer X agreed to build on the lot a structure to the taxpayer's specifications. The taxpayer was responsible for all transaction costs and carrying costs. The construction was financed by a mortgage and a note guaranteed by the taxpayer and was nonrecourse to taxpayer X. The taxpayer assumed personal liability for the note and mortgage at the time property A was exchanged for property B in its improved state.

The IRS challenged the transactions and determined that actual transaction was a sale of property A to taxpayer X.

The Court agreed with the IRS because.......

Though this appears to be a reverse exchange, it occurred prior to the issuance of Rev Proc 2000-37 which provides a safe harbor for reverse exchanges. Therefore Rev Proc 2000-37 does not apply.

The taxpayer did not locate and simply identify property B as potential replacement property for property A. The taxpayer <u>purchased it</u> without the participation of an exchange facilitator a year or more prior to his intention to build and occupy. He then transferred title, subject to a reacquisition agreement, and at the same time obligated himself to relinquish property A.

The Court looked to the 3 month ownership period of property B by taxpayer X to determine if taxpayer X had received all of the benefits and burdens of ownership. The Court determined that taxpayer X acquired no equity interest in property B, it made no economic outlay to acquire property B, it was not at risk to any extent because it's obligation and security interest was no recourse. Taxpayer X was only obligated to reconvey the improved property B to the taxpayer pursuant to a prearrangement the taxpayer was obligated to take and pay for.

The Court determined that the real economic transaction occurred when the taxpayer transferred title of property A to X in exchange for $142,400 which actually occurred at the time of the 'second' closing.

Interesting points in this case......

The exchange facilitator or intermediary was bypassed.

The taxpayer already owned the land he wished to build on - you cannot exchange real property for an improvement made on another piece of real estate you already own

The taxpayer failed to transfer all of the benefits and burdens of ownership to the other party but by agreement retained those benefits and burdens.

Lesson in this case.........

Use an experienced Intermediary or Accommodator

Case #4
Florida Industries Investment Corporation
v. Commissioner
KTC 2001-164

Summary

This exchange began in 1990 before the safe harbor was enacted on June 10, 1991. An Escrow

Agreement was the backbone of the exchange and a business associate of many years served as the Escrow Agent. Many of the requirements contained in the safe harbor rules were contained in the Escrow Agreement.

This exchange began to fail on the day after it began. The Escrow Agent sent approximately $30,000 more to closing on the replacement than was needed. The money was not returned to escrow.

The exchanger closed on several properties that were not identified within 45 days as required in the Escrow Agreement. One of the properties was the primary residence of the exchanger's only shareholder. The Escrow Agent authorized two checks to be issued before the stipulated 180 day exchange period had expired. One check was payable to the exchanger and another to a sister corporation.

The Internal Revenue Service challenged the exchange. They determined the taxpayer had dominion and control over the escrowed funds. They declared the exchange to be a sale and repurchase of property not of a like-kind.

The Tax Court agreed with the IRS and the Appellate Court affirmed the decision.

The courts agreed because……….

The $30,000 was not returned to escrow, there was no record of any replacement property having been identified and the exchanger's shareholder prepared one of the checks signed by the Escrow Agent.

Interesting points in this case ....

The exchanger went to great lengths to have an escrow agreement prepared. The agreement contained all of the language, stipulations and restraints the IRS was looking for when it examined 1031 exchanges.

The exchanger appears to have ignored all of the requirements set out in the escrow agreement.

Lesson in this case......

Don't shortcut your exchange or accommodation agreement. The wording is there to protect your exchange.

A Great Scenario... Definitely not a court case....

At least not yet.....................

Dick and Jane are husband and wife. They own a home in California (only in California can this happen). They have owned the home for 12 years and it has $1,000,000 in Capital gain. They also own 2 rental properties each of which have more than $500,000 in Capital gain.

Dick and Jane are not happy and decided to divorce. In their divorce settlement, they agree to hold the family home and each will take one of the rental properties. Jane and her personal trainer marry and move into her rental property. They live there for two years and decide to sell the property. They, as joint taxpayers, claim the primary residence exclusion of $500,000 and move into the marital home.

Dick and the former aupair agree to marry. They live in the family home for 2 years and then move into the other rental property.

During the third year that Jane and her personal trainer are living in the family home, Dick and Jane decide to sell the property since the children are now in college. The property sold and each couple elected to exclude $500,000 of gain on the sale of a primary residence. They meet the exclusion requirements because each couple lived in the residence for two of the five years immediately prior to the sale and at least one member of each couple was an owner of the property for 2 of the 5 years immediately prior to sale.

Dick and his Aupair sell the other rental property 2 years later and they exclude $500,000 (joint) in capital gain on the sale of their primary residence.

So, with good planning each of these taxpayers managed to exclude $2,000,000 from taxation over a 7 year period.

Oddly enough, the new law regarding primary residences allows this. For how long remains to be seen............?

Happy Exchanging

About the Author

Bettye Matthews is a certified public accountant licensed in both Florida and Maryland. Her first experience with §1031 tax deferred exchanges came as an instructor with the Adult Education Division of the University of Maryland. As an instructor, Ms. Matthews facilitated discussions concerning the effect of taxation on real estate. At that time the "Safe Harbor" discussed in this handbook was not available and exchanges were a tedious, dangerous and expensive undertaking.

Mrs. Matthews is currently the President and CEO of Exchange Professionals, Inc. in Westminster, Maryland. The company provides Qualified Intermediary and Accommodator services to real estate investors.

For lists of other Qualified Intermediaries throughout the country, check the web site of The Federation of Exchange Accommodators at www.1031.org.

www.ingramcontent.com/pod-product-compliance
Lightning Source LLC
Chambersburg PA
CBHW032024170526
45157CB00002B/845